THE MASK OF POLITICS

Maurice Cranston

The Mask of Politics
and other essays

THE LIBRARY

Distributed by
OPEN COURT
Publishing Co.
La Salle, Ill. 61301

800-435-6850 or 815-223-2521

First published 1973 in the United States of America by
The Library Press, New York

International Standard Book Number: 0-912050-36-5
Library of Congress Catalog Card Number: 72-7969

Printed in Great Britain by
Ebenezer Baylis and Son Limited
The Trinity Press, Worcester, and London

Contents

Acknowledgements

The author wishes to acknowledge the permission to reprint granted by the editors and publishers of the journals in which these essays originally appeared, namely: *Encounter* Ltd, The Bodley Head, London, and The Library Press, New York, for 'The Pessimism of Herbert Marcuse' (originally published as 'Herbert Marcuse'); *Encounter*, Ltd for 'Camus and Justice' (originally published as 'Albert Camus'); *Encounter* Ltd, for 'Michel Foucault: A structuralist view of reason and madness' (originally published as 'Michel Foucault'); Penguin Books Ltd, Harmondsworth and Baltimore, for 'Rousseau's Social Contract' (originally published as an introduction to a translation of Rousseau's *Social Contract*); *Encounter* Ltd, for 'Sartre and Violence'.

'The Mask of Politics' is a revised version of an inaugural lecture entitled 'Ethics and Politics', published by Weidenfeld and Nicolson for the London School of Economics, and by *Encounter* Ltd.

'Some Aspects of the History of Freedom' was originally published in *Theorie und Politik: Festschrift zum 70. Geburtstag für Carl Joachim Friedrich*, edited by Klaus von Beyme (Martinus Nijhoff, The Hague).

Grateful thanks are addressed to all the foregoing persons and institutions.

The essays which appear in this book have been written over the past ten years. Most of them were first published in *Encounter*, and several of them take the form of critical studies of contemporary political thinkers. All these essays are concerned, in one way or another, with the defence of freedom and moderation in politics, against the destructive intrusion of ideology, whether of the left or right.

London   M.C.

The Mask of
Politics

What is politics? There was a time when anyone who raised this question would be expected to give a definition of the word 'politics'. If this expectation still exists, I fear I shall disappoint it. For one thing, most of us already know what we mean by politics, and we gain little by looking up the definitions provided in books by academic theorists: in such places, we read, for example, that 'politics is the authoritative allocation of values in a community' (David Easton),[1] 'politics is the struggle for power' (Max Weber),[2] 'politics is a systematic effort to move other men in the pursuit of some design' (Bertrand de Jouvenel),[3] or 'politics is who gets what, when, how' (Harold Lasswell).[4] None of these sounds right: for the reason, I believe, that none of them *is* right. They do not correspond to what we find when we look at that complex activity known as politics. For what is it that people who take up politics actually do?

First of all, they talk. It has always surprised me that Professor Michael Oakeshott, in making the point that politics is a practice, compared it to the art of cookery.[5] For surely if politics is an art, it is one of the performing arts, and not one of the creative ones. Plato noticed this when he compared the politician to the flute-player. But

1. David Easton, *The Political System*, New York, Knopf, 1953, p. 129.

2. Max Weber, *Politik als Beruf* (quoted by G. E. G. Catlin in J. A. Gould and V. V. Thursby, ed., *Contemporary Political Thought*, New York, Holt, Rinehart and Winston, 1969, p. 27).

3. Bertrand de Jouvenel, *The Pure Theory of Politics*, Cambridge University Press, 1963, p. 30.

4. Harold D. Lasswell, *Politics: Who Gets What, When, How*, New York, McGraw-Hill, 1936.

5. Michael Oakeshott, *Rationalism in Politics*, London, Methuen, 1962, p. 119.

the flute-player is not right either. As a performer, the politician is theatrical, not musical. The world of politics is undoubtedly a stage, and every politician is an actor on it. By this I mean no disrespect. It seems to me a pity that the word 'theatrical' should have become a pejorative one, as it undoubtedly has. It might be worth pausing to consider why. The most thoroughgoing attack on the theatre that I know of is the one that Rousseau makes in his *Lettre à Monsieur d'Alembert*. In this letter, Rousseau depicts the theatre as an evil institution with no saving grace or merit, and the métier of the actor as a totally corrupt one. A word that recurs often in this letter is the word 'representation'. Rousseau attacks the theatre because fictions and falsehoods are represented on the stage as realities. In his *Social Contract*,[1] he translates this hatred of representation in dramatic art into a hatred of representation in parliamentary government. Readers will remember his argument that representatives or deputies do not, and cannot represent the people who elect them. As soon as they are elected, Rousseau says, the representatives become the rulers. And the people, instead of ruling themselves, are enslaved by the deputies they have voted for. This is the basis of Rousseau's belief that representative government is fraudulent. Dramatic art he considers an evil for other, but equally striking reasons.

About half-way through his *Lettre à Monsieur d'Alembert*, Rousseau asks: 'What is the talent of an actor?' He answers: 'The art of counterfeit: the art of assuming a personality other than his own, of appearing different from what he is, simulating passion while his feelings are cold, of saying something he does not believe just as naturally as if he really believed it.'[2]

Conscious, perhaps, that these words might put the reader in mind at once of politicians, Rousseau hastens to add that there should be no confusing the actor and the orator:

The difference between the two is very great. When the orator presents himself to the public it is to make a speech, and not to put on an act; he represents no one but himself; he fulfils only his own role; he speaks in his

1. J-J. Rousseau, *The Social Contract*, trans. M. Cranston, Penguin Classics, 1968, book III, chs. 10 and 15.

2. *J-J. Rousseau, Citoyen de Genève, à Monsieur d'Alembert*, Amsterdam, Rey, 1758, p. 143.

own name alone; he does not say, nor should he say, anything other than what he thinks; the man and the *persona* are identical; he is where he should be, and he discharges the same duty which any other citizen in his place would discharge.[1]

I do not think one needs to make any detailed comparison between Rousseau's uncharitable description of the actor and his flattering description of the orator to see that neither his criticism of the one nor his praise of the other is altogether fair. For if a man offers, as an actor does, what is plainly declared to be an imitation, it is unreasonable to complain that what he offers is an imitation. And, correspondingly, it is no praise of actual orators to protest that *the* orator, namely the ideal image of an orator, is a man who is wholly and patently sincere. And, indeed, if Rousseau had based his conception of the orator on a consideration of the orator's role in the real world, he might have given us a different picture.

The political speaker is not simply a citizen who stands up artlessly and says what he has in mind. The orator is a man whose function is to persuade his hearers to accept, or agree to or approve of a certain policy. And this is an intricate art, which requires both natural talent and some professional formation. The calling of the politician is one that deserves a great deal of respect, and I think Rousseau does no service to him by praising him for qualities that he does not possess. Rousseau is unfair to the actor in attributing to him faults which cannot logically be considered faults: and he is unfair to the orator, in ascribing to him virtues which it would be foolish to expect him to have.

The life of politics is an arduous one. A man who chooses it is continuously put to the test. He has to satisfy other people time and time again. He has no security of tenure, as a civil servant or a professor has. A politician can never be sure how popular he is, although he soon knows when he is not wanted. Even the humblest member of a legislative body like the House of Commons has to satisfy his party leadership, his constituency committee and the voters. Any one of these groups has the power to dismiss him. So he cannot simply speak spontaneously; his speeches have to measure

1. Ibid., p. 146.

the demands and the expectations of all these very different people. Like an actor, he must know how to please and persuade and engage the sympathies of others. If he is to succeed he must be dedicated to his calling, and no matter how great his native gift he must master the techniques of public debate and public relations; he must even look after his looks.

If politicians talk, they also, of course, decide, legislate, vote, pass resolutions and settle the rules that we ordinary people have to observe. But politicians do not do all these things in public. There are many textbooks about 'decision-making' and 'decision theory', but this is in fact one of the least known parts of political life. We know who votes where in Parliament in response to that very theatrical device, the division bell. But we do not know how Ministers speak and vote in the Cabinet, or what discussions go on between leading members of the opposition party. In the theatre of politics the curtain is firmly rung down from time to time, and a large and extremely important part of the drama is enacted in secret.

It is frustrating for political science that political life is so sensitive to observation. For either a politician is exceedingly conscious of an audience, and addresses himself to it whenever he speaks; or he makes sure that all observers are excluded. In the one case he is thinking all the time of the effect his words are having; in the other, he takes care that his words shall be heard only by his colleagues and their confidential staff. For this reason the political scientist whose modest desire is to observe what we like to call the political process has the choice of joining the audience and being talked at, or putting his ear to a hole in the curtain, and finding it firmly blocked. Of course there are records from the past, but that only means that the political scientist becomes a kind of contemporary historian. And perhaps that is what political science, for the most part, is: a felicitous union of history and philosophy, for us as it was for Aristotle.

Politicians, perhaps, do more important work than actors: but why does Rousseau insist so much on the moral distinction between the two? The explanation may be connected with the strong feelings that Rousseau had about the disjunction between appearance and reality. He considered appearance to be the domain of deception and therefore bad, whereas reality was the province of truth, and therefore good. The theatre was bad because it was an admitted temple of illusions. The political forum, on the other hand, was good, for it was there that men assumed the full reality of citizens. Conceiving appearance and reality thus to be antithetical Rousseau could never fully understand the life of politics, where appearance is almost as important as reality, is even indeed a part of it.

Rousseau demanded sincerity, rather as existentialists of more recent times demand authenticity. And this is something far in excess of what we can fairly demand of any political speaker. We expect our orator to be consistent in what he says, to sound as if he believed it, both to be and to appear at least moderately honest. But we do not expect him always to speak as if he were on oath. Franklin Roosevelt was a very worthy statesman, but no one who reads his letters, with their assurances of affection to any Tom, Dick or Harry who might help to get him nominated and elected President, can believe that Roosevelt was wholly sincere in what he wrote. Perhaps a man who wrote letters like this in private life might incur our criticism, but politics is *not* private life, and we must introduce different considerations when we judge it. The options that are available to a man in politics are often very limited, and the risks attached to each of the several courses open to him may be almost equally great. It is easy for the critic, and especially for the scholar, to condemn his failings. Lord Attlee was once heard to say to an academic person who was telling him how to run his government: 'If a politician makes an ass of himself, he loses his seat; but a professor who makes an ass of himself is never going to lose his chair.' It is not at all easy for the politician to be wise – or even to be sure what is right and wrong. A private person who is constantly straight, frank, open, scrupulous, and morally transparent is a man we wholeheartedly admire. More precisely, he is a man we would wholeheartedly admire, for such men are not altogether common. But what if a statesman exhibits similar qualities?

One of the things that helped to make Machiavelli a Machiavellian was the experience of watching Piero Soderini enact the role of *gonfaloniere* of Florence. Soderini was a man of intense, unyielding and high moral principles. The result of his behaving with scrupulous and impeccable justice towards the Spaniards was that the Spanish army invaded the Florentine town of Prato and committed hideous atrocities. Machiavelli drew from this the lesson that the statesman should not allow his dealings with other states always to be governed by the same moral scruples that governed the dealings of private persons. It is often said that Machiavelli introduced the idea of a politics without morality. I disagree. His argument, on the contrary, seems to me to be that there is only one true morality: but that the ruler must sometimes disregard it. Machiavelli's words are that the ruler 'should not depart from what is morally right if he can observe it, but should know how to adopt what is bad when he is obliged to'.[1] Machiavelli makes no pretence that the bad is anything other than bad. He says that bad things must be done by rulers, but only very sparingly, and then in a manner which is as much concealed as possible. Like Rousseau, Machiavelli dwells on the distinction between appearance and reality. But unlike Rousseau, Machiavelli attaches value to the appearance of virtue as well as to the practice of it. He tells his prince that he 'should know how to appear compassionate, trustworthy, humane, honest and religious, and actually *be* so, but yet he should have his mind so trained that when it is necessary he can become the contrary'.[2]

This suggestion opens the door to the alarming and indeed wrongful doctrine of the *raison d'état*, but even those of us who deplore it must surely admit that Machiavelli has made an important point here. Since a ruler has to deal with other rulers who are sometimes rapacious and unscrupulous, he cannot easily always observe the same moral law which should govern the conduct of individuals within a civilized community. But at the same time, it is his duty as the head of one such civilized community to uphold the moral law. So even if he has sometimes to contravene the principles of that morality, he cannot let his willingness be known. It is not only that a

1. *Il Principe*, ed. L. A. Burd, Oxford University Press, 1891, ch. 18, p. 305.
2. *Idem*. For a valuable discussion of this point, see Sheldon Wolin, *Politics and Vision*, Boston: Little, Brown and Co.; London: Allen and Unwin, 1961, ch. VII, pp. 195–238.

reputation for deceit makes it hard for a man to deceive successfully. There is another consideration. A ruler or *principe* is a prominent person. If he bears visible witness to the notion that deceit is sometimes permissible, other people are only too likely to follow his example in their private lives. And this is something that Machiavelli has no wish to bring about. No one should be given any excuse or encouragement to be bad, just because the *principe*, in the cause of duty, is sometimes obliged to be bad.

The world judges by appearances, if only because appearance is all the world has got to judge by. If one recalls the men who have been banished from British public life for moral turpitude in the past hundred years or so – of Sir Charles Dilke, for example, or Parnell – the reason for their fall was plainly the open scandal rather than their sinful deeds, for the same kind of sinful deeds, we have since learned from the biographies, were being done by men more prominent in the kingdom than Dilke or Parnell. The difficulty is that once the sinful deed has been exposed, others in authority dare not allow themselves to appear to condone it, so they are swift to punish a man for doing things they themselves have done, but effectively concealed. One of the reasons for the enduring hostility of rulers, and politicians generally, towards Machiavelli is that he advises them to do consciously and deliberately what many of them already do naturally, and prefer not to think about. However, Machiavelli never explicitly authorized the use of deception for the protection of politicians' careers; he authorized the use of deception rather for the concealment of those necessary acts of state which violate morality.

The curious thing is that even Rousseau himself, when he thinks most earnestly about the possibilities that politics affords, himself not only excuses insincerity, but positively recommends it. When he writes in *The Social Contract* about the most important *orateur* of all, the law-giver, the founder of the republic, he says that the orator must not speak in his own words to the public, because the vulgar do not understand the language of the learned. He urges the law-giver to have recourse to dissimulation, and to suggest to the crowd that the proposals he himself has devised have been laid down by the deity, 'thus', as Rousseau puts it, 'compelling by divine authority persons who cannot be moved by human prudence'.[1]

Readers of Rousseau's *Emile* may remember rather similar deceits and stratagems being employed by Emile's tutor to bring up the boy in the path of virtue. So Rousseau cannot be said to have consistently believed that sincerity, authenticity, transparency is always imperative in either private or public life. Indeed if frankness is to be the virtue that we are going to set such store by, Rousseau is plainly inferior to Machiavelli. For what Rousseau has done is to insinuate by the back door the principle of dissimulation he has rejected at the front. What Machiavelli has done, paradoxically, is to strip from the ruler the very veils that he is telling the ruler to wear.

Of the two Machiavelli is in many ways the more sympathetic moralist. And if it seems to a reader perverse to apply the word 'moralist' to a man who plainly says that the ruler cannot always be moral, then such a reader can only be referred to the vast literature which exists in the Christian Church on the subject of casuistry. Or if that is too daunting an undertaking, I will simply cite the late Dean of Lichfield's biography of Archbishop William Temple, where Dr Iremonger judges Dr Temple to have been too kind, loving and chaste a man to be an effective headmaster of an English public school.[2] If a clergyman thus considers purity of soul a handicap in the field of Christian education, can we reproach Machiavelli for considering rigidity of moral scruples a handicap in government and diplomacy?

To assert that there are certain exceptions in the application of the moral law, is by no means to deny – but rather to affirm, that the moral law has a general application: and a general application so compelling that any exception to it needs careful justification and very delicate concealment. It was certainly no part of Machiavelli's scheme to separate politics from morals, or to contemplate politics

---

1. *The Social Contract* (*op. cit.*), p. 87. It is interesting to note that Rousseau fortifies this recommendation in his text with a quotation, in the footnotes, from Machiavelli's *Discorsi*, V, xi; 'The truth is that there has never been in any country an extraordinary legislator who has not invoked the deity, for otherwise his laws would not have been accepted.'

2. F. A. Iremonger, *William Temple*, Oxford University Press, 1948, pp. 144–6.

in the light of a science from which all normative factors were removed. That was to be the enterprise of a much later generation.

Politicians talk. But has politics a language of its own? It has certainly not a distinctively technical language, as most trades and professions have. In phonetics, for example, there are technical terms like 'fricative', 'sonorant' and 'vocalic' which are used in a specific way and which apprentices in the subject have to learn. Of course there are also words that 'belong', so to speak, to politics: words like 'democratic', 'free', 'just', 'legitimate' and so on, but far from the application of these words being settled by convention, it is just these things that are argued over. In phonetics there is general agreement as to which speech sounds shall be classified, for example, as fricative; but there is no agreement in politics as to which states shall be classified as democratic. An even more important difference is that the word 'fricative' in phonetics implies no evaluation of good or bad. It is simply a neutral technical term. The word 'democratic', by contrast, is loaded with evaluative content. In the 1930s and earlier many people detested democracy, and they spoke the word with a voice of disapprobation; on the other hand, many people esteemed democracy, and they invested the word with their sense of approval. It was a highly controversial word. More recently this has changed, and 'democracy' has become a word of commendation, virtually throughout the world, although it is certainly not the case that what was most commonly thought of as democracy before the war has been universally adopted.

And yet the dictionary definition of the word has not changed. The latest editions give the same report on usage as the old editions: democracy is a 'system of government by the people'. But where are these systems to be found? Some theorists say that democracy is the kind of government that is practised in America, so that all you have to do, to learn about democracy, is to study American government at work. Others direct our attention to the people's democracies, such as the German Democratic Republic or the Democratic Republic of North Korea. There are those who say that the only vestiges of democracy left in the modern world are to be found in Switzerland. Then, by way of contrast, there is Professor C. B. Macpherson, who has argued that we can find democracy alike in capitalist and communist and underdeveloped countries, although it assumes in those places a variety of forms.[1] Professor Macpherson has thus succeeded where Woodrow Wilson failed: he has made the world safe for democracy by the adroit device of proposing that almost all known forms of government may be classified as democratic.

Of course they all want to be, and we ought not to be surprised that once a word has become a universal prestige word, as 'democracy' has become, that everyone should claim it. The problem that falls to political philosophy is to ask whether any criteria can be invoked to judge the claim of a given system to be a democratic one. If 'democratic' is a word which has become more laudatory with the passage of time, there are other words we hear in political talk which have become increasingly pejorative. Think of the word 'bourgeois'. The dictionary meaning of this has never changed: to be bourgeois is to belong to the town-dwelling middle class as distinct from the nobility, the peasantry and the working class. It is the class to which most of us belong. So naturally it has no glamour for us. And yet in its earlier use, the word 'bourgeois' was spoken with esteem, even by people like Voltaire. The nobility seems habitually to have used it with scorn – as we might expect – and we could well understand the peasantry and the working class doing so too. But the peculiar thing is that the bourgeois class has itself taken to using the word with as much implied hostility as the other classes. Everyone has turned out to agree that 'bourgeois' is bad. If a man stood for election in a conspicuously bourgeois constituency such as Bournemouth or Kensington or Cheltenham, and said 'Protect the bourgeoisie' he would not earn a single vote, but he might do quite well if he said 'Protect the middle classes'.

Yet, from a certain point of view, he would be saying the same thing. But not from the point of view of politics. In the one case he would be employing a word so loaded with miscellaneous disapprobation that it is political folly to use it. In the other case he would be using a word which the majority of voters would hear with kindly recognition. From the point of view of politics, the most important

1. C. B. Macpherson, *The Real World of Democracy*, Oxford University Press, 1966.

feature of the word 'bourgeois' is that it has become contaminated. With the passage of time, some of the words we use become degraded and some become elevated. And a political speaker has to be alert to these changes, if he is to make use of words persuasively.

Some changes happen quickly. Consider, for example, the word 'sovereignty'. Thirty years ago this was a word in low repute in England. Harold Laski was only one of several who suggested that sovereignty was a concept that should be banished altogether.[1] Even as short a time ago as 1969, Professor W. J. Stankiewicz published a book called *In Defense of Sovereignty*[2] because he felt that the concept needed rehabilitation. But more recently in England the word 'sovereignty' has been used without hesitation as the name of a cherished principle. Even some of Laski's own political disciples objected to the idea of Great Britain joining the Common Market because, they said, it would 'infringe the national sovereignty'. A word which seemed only twenty-five years ago to give off an unpleasing odour of nationalistic narrowness, has since been invested once more with the proud spirit of British independence.

Or consider the word 'violence'. Until a few years ago, this word was invoked only as a word of condemnation. Its use implied the presence of excessive or unjustified force. Both in moral theory and ordinary conversation, the distinction between force and violence was plainly understood. Force was something always regrettable but in certain circumstances permissible. The word 'force' had no judgement of condemnation built into it as the word 'violence' had. We might have said: 'He used force and was wrong to do so.' But we would not have said 'He used violence and was wrong to do so', because that would be to utter a pleonasm. 'Violence' was wrong by definition.

Recently this seems to have changed; and we even find 'violence' used as a word of praise. What used to be called force is now called violence. Sometimes this is done deliberately, as by Sartre, for example, who argues that violence is what lies behind all civil society,

1. Harold J. Laski, *The Grammar of Politics*, London, Allen and Unwin; 4th edn 1938; pp. 64–5.
2. W. J. Stankiewicz, *In Defense of Sovereignty*, New York, Oxford University Press, 1969.

and who would like to see violence used to institute a revolution. And whereas there is permissible force and wrongful force in traditional thinking, for Sartre there is bad violence or good violence. Although only a few people subscribe to Sartre's political theory, or even perhaps understand it, many people nowadays have taken to using the word 'violence' as he does. Admittedly, 'violence' is used in a laudatory way in the writings of several minor political theorists who flourished before the war: but such theorists used to be thought of fascistic, and indeed it was long regarded as the badge of a fascist to speak in praise of violence. Even as ruthless a tyrant as Stalin never admitted to use of anything other than force.

Now it is becoming increasingly accepted that 'violence' may be used either as a neutral or a laudatory word.[1] This may well mean that the fascist ethos is coming to life again: but it also serves to remind us that words – and especially the words we use in politics – can gain prestige as well as lose it, and that the normative implications of a word are never fixed and precise. If we examine the to-and-fro of political debate we may notice how words, and even whole phrases are picked up from one speaker by another, picked up even from an antagonist in the debate, and used by that speaker to his own advantage. Some phrase-maker, for example, introduces a fanciful expression, such as 'equality of opportunity' as something he wants to recommend. It sounds good. It is taken up by speakers of all parties. And before long everyone is declaring that equality of opportunity is what we all want – a great national ideal.

This is the kind of euphoria which political philosophy tends to spoil. For it asks such questions as: what sense can we make of this so-called principle? The two words concerned contradict one another: for the concept of opportunity is logically connected with competitive disparity of advantage, whereas the concept of equality is logically connected with parity of advantage, so it is far from clear what their union could possibly signify. Of course the word 'equality'

---

1. And not only in pamphleteering or journalism. The word is used in this manner in several papers presented at the conference of the Institut International de Philosophie Politique at Colmar, July 1971, on the general theme of *La Violence*. These papers will be published by the Presses Universitaires de France, Paris, in an edition prepared by Robert Derathé.

is keenly appreciated on the left, and the word 'opportunity' is much cherished on the right: and a phrase which exploits the prestige of both may well appeal to a large public, if only at the expense of both sides accepting a loss of definition, allowing the concepts to become blurred and soft and nebulous. This may not be an undesired result. In politics there is a tendency for speakers to adopt a yielding, feminine attitude to words, a posture which favours the use of them in a slack and unexacting way. Journalism does nothing to halt the process. Indeed the phrase-maker is a creature who flourishes more on the margin of politics than in politics itself. Sir Norman Angell once wrote a book called *The Great Illusion*. It argued that war brought victors no gain. A few years after it was published the 1914 war broke out, and Norman Angell's 'great illusion' proved to be itself an illusion. But that did not hinder the success of the book. Norman Angell was venerated as a sage, knighted and awarded the Nobel Prize. We may perhaps remark a parallel case in Professor Kenneth Galbraith's *The Affluent Society*: a year or two after its publication, developments in the American economy refuted one by one the more important tenets of Galbraith's diagnosis. But never mind, *The Affluent Society*, like *The Great Illusion*, was already a classic. In the realm of pamphleteering the title is everything, and the unforgettable titles keep rolling off the press: *The Second Sex*, *The Divided Self*, *The Naked Ape*, *The Female Eunuch*, *The One-Dimensional Man* – glittering phrases that win for their authors a place in the immortality of folklore.[1]

But politics is not the same as pamphleteering. The pamphleteer is never called upon to answer for his words, whereas a politician who makes a phrase that proves strikingly inept will have it hurled against him, again and again. Think of Neville Chamberlain and his 'peace for our time', or President Johnson and his 'great society', or Mr Harold Wilson's 'The pound in your pocket is not worth a penny

1. J. K. Galbraith, *The Affluent Society*, Hamish Hamilton, 1958; Simone de Beauvoir, *The Second Sex*, trans. H. M. Parshley, Cape, 1968; R. D. Laing, *The Divided Self*, Tavistock, 1960; Penguin, 1970; Desmond Morris, *The Naked Ape*, Cape, 1967; Corgi, 1969; G. Greer, *The Female Eunuch*, Granada (Paladin), 1971; H. Marcuse, *The One-Dimensional Man*, Beacon Press and Routledge, 1964; Sphere 1970.

less', not to mention Mr Heath's election words about bringing down the prices of the contents of the shopping basket. A memorable phrase can be disastrous, for the simple reason that it is remembered. A politician has good reason to be nervous of words, and to want to soften all those sharp edges, in case they cut him. It is part of the task of political philosophy to tryto recover that dreaded clarity.

The twentieth century, among its many other disagreeable characteristics, has been an age of dogma. The eighteenth century doubted, the nineteenth century believed, but the twentieth century knows – or rather it thinks it knows. Among the dogmas which have informed the thinking of our century there are two that have a particular importance. The first asserts that statements of fact are so totally distinct from judgements of value that there can be no question of deriving one from the other. The thought behind this dogma is not new. It was suggested, with a particular intention, by David Hume in the eighteenth century. It was repeated in different contexts in the nineteenth century. And there is no denying, that in its limited formulation, it is true: statements of fact *are* logically distinct from judgements of value, and for purposes of analysis we must take them apart. But what the twentieth century has elevated into a dogma is the further assertion that there can be no rational fusion of fact and value or any logical derivation of judgements of value from statements of fact. In the past few years, this dogma has lost much of its hold on people's minds. Recent work in ethics has done a good deal to discredit it. Several methods have been demonstrated by which judgements of value can be logically derived from statements of fact.[1] The analysis of language has shown that the function of certain words is to be at the same time both descriptive and evaluative.

The other dogma which has informed so much theorizing in the twentieth century is the dogma of the identity of determinism and human freedom. This derives from the suggestion put forward by

1. See, for example, Alasdair MacIntyre, *Against the Self-Images of the Age*, London, Sidgwick and Jackson, 1971; W. D. Hudson, ed., *The Is-Ought Question*, London, Macmillan, 1969; Charles Taylor, *The Explanation of Behaviour*, London, Routledge, 1964.

Hobbes and Locke that there is no such problem as the free will problem, on the grounds that there is no antithesis between determinism and freedom, men's actions being at the same time both determined and free. On the basis of this dogma, twentieth-century investigators have directed their research into the explanation of human behaviour as a search for determining causes, and the study of man has become no different in kind from the study of rats. This second dogma, too, has lost a good deal of its hold in the past year or two. The case against determinism has been put from so many different points of view in philosophy that hardly anything remains to be said in support of it. It has even been accepted by the more sophisticated champions of Marxism, and what was once presented as a form of scientific historicism is now put forward as a form of libertarian metaphysics.

Nevertheless, these two dogmas – the divorce of fact and value, and the marriage of freedom and determinism – have both been incorporated into positivism, the doctrine which has shaped so much of the thought and even the culture of our time. This is a doctrine which has taken various forms, and each with its own bearing on theorizing about politics. An early and influential type was legal positivism. This, of course, is the doctrine that law is the system of rules and penalties which is actually enforced in any state. Law, as one theorist put it, is fact. Law is the code which is actually imposed by the courts and the authorities, as distinct from any ideal code, which ought, or should be upheld. Legal positivists, therefore, dispute the traditional understanding of natural law as being the supreme law. For them natural law is no part of law at all. It is either philosophy or nonsense, which, from the point of view of positivism are not very different.

Legal positivism rests squarely on the dogma of the mutual impenetrability of fact and value. In asserting that law is fact, the legal positivist assumes that he is denying that law is value. What his dogma forbids him to see, is what anyone must see who reflects on law as a system: that justice is an integral part of the system which constitutes law. Justice is part of the meaning of the word 'law'. Law is both normative and factual. And in this respect it is very like politics.

Another form of positivism which has had a great vogue in the twentieth century is historical positivism, the belief that history is a science, a science dedicated to the search for facts and the discovery of the causes of past events and movements through the observation of regularities in what is called historical phenomena. In the positivist dream, the historian is a man who records facts without judging them, and then, as a scientist, goes on to discover the cause of things. Since human choices and decisions are seen as part of a succession of cause and effect, positivist historians think it is just as sensible to look for the cause of the French Revolution as it is an engineer to look for the cause of an explosion in the cellar.

This enterprise in historical scholarship coincided with another, more extensive one, that of positivistic social science. Again the divorce of fact and value was duly proclaimed. Social science was to stay in the realm of fact: in the elegant German word of Max Weber, it was to be *wertfrei*. It was also going to discover the causes of things – the causes, not so much past events, as the positivistic historians did, but of movements and changes in society generally. It was going to do for society what the natural scientists had done for nature. It was going to discover laws. Some of the laws they produced have to do with politics. For instance, there was Robert Michels's 'iron law of oligarchy', the law that a minority will always prevail over the majority. Some readers may not think this law any great improvement on Rousseau's observation that the ministers of a state will always tend to turn themselves from the servants into the masters of the people, but at least we may admit that Robert Michels adds something to the iron law of oligarchy: he adds the iron. But we must not be frivolous: for the sober truth of the matter is that the formulations of theorists like Michels had a great influence on the development of political science. It inspired after the First World War an attempt to reform, or revolutionize, political science in the same positivist lines, something which was spoken of at the time as the endeavour to transform political science into a 'genuine science'.[1] Once more the two dogmas were repeated. Political

1. See, among the many publications on this subject: G. E. G. Catlin, *The Science and Method of Politics*, New York, Shoe String Press, 1926; B. R. Crick, *The American Science of Politics*, University of California Press, 1959; H. Eulau, *The Behavioural Persuasion*, New York, Random House, 1963;

science must stick to facts and banish values. And it must look for the causes of things, the causes, that is, of political behaviour, through the collection of data, the observation of regularities and the formulation of general laws.

This now seems a rather old-fashioned, as well as a defective account of what a science is: but at the time it found a response. And positivist political science took root and thrived in America, taking over more and more political science departments in the ever-expanding North American universities. The tradition of Aristotle was discarded. The history of political ideas, political theory and history, even the study of institutions and laws was pushed aside by this new aggressive science, whose aim according to one of its most noted exponents, Professor Robert Dahl, was to state 'all the phenomena of government in terms of observed and observable behaviour of men'.[1] It was then that we first heard talk of eliminating political philosophy.

But if positivist political science flourished in America, it soon changed its nature in the process. It began to claim a different identity from that with which it started out. In the writings of its exponents which date from the 1920s and the 1930s, the gospel of the *wertfrei*, empirical and objective social science is reiterated. But in the 1940s, American political science assumes the guise of a policy science in the service of democracy. One of the best and liveliest of the American political scientists, Professor Harold Lasswell, suggested that political science was as much directed to the defence of democracy as was military science itself.[2] Plainly such a science is not value-free, whatever else it may be.

There is a well-known article on Lasswell by Professor David Easton,[3] which suggests that Lasswell's work was never really

A. F. Bentley, *The Process of Government*, Evanston, 1935; S. Rice, *Quantitative Methods in Politics*, New York, 1928.

1. Robert Dahl, 'The behavioral approach', *American Political Science Review*, lv, no. 4, December 1961, p. 763.

2. Harold Lasswell, *Democracy Through Public Opinion*, Menasha, Wisc., 1941. 'The emergency affords a remarkable opportunity for the moral defense of America' (p. 175).

3. David Easton, 'Harold Lasswell', *Journal of Politics*, xii, no. 3, August 1950, p. 450.

value-free. Easton argues that Lasswell's early work rests on a veiled acceptance of the élitist values of Pareto and Robert Michels and that the real difference between Lasswell's earlier and later work is that he renounced this unavowed acceptance of élitism in favour of an avowed acceptance of the values of democracy. But there is another characteristic of Harold Lasswell's early work, which may be more important than any veiled adhesion to élitism, and that is the kind of science which Lasswell had in mind when he spoke of science: for this is something he shared with other practitioners of behavioural political science. The kind of science which served as their model was not physics, but psychopathology, a science which is itself deeply permeated by conceptions of value. So 'science' in Aristotle's sense had been abandoned only to make way for 'science' in Freud's sense. Psychopathology is a therapeutic science, interested not only in facts, but equally, and indeed primarily, concerned with such conceptions as cure, normality, health, satisfaction, adjustment and so forth. There is nothing *wertfrei* here.

A very large part of positivist political science in America was based from the beginning on this therapeutic model, so that when American political science proclaimed itself in the 1940s to be a 'policy science' it was not so much changing its nature, as becoming aware of its real nature. Of course, not every social science positivist has followed this pattern of transforming their subject into a therapeutic enterprise. One leading behavioural psychologist, Professor B. F. Skinner of Harvard, has attacked what he calls 'the medical analogy' and the prevailing tendency of social science to think of the problems of men in society as the problems of patients needing cure. But Skinner can hardly be said to have remained true to the ideal of a *wertfrei* social science. In his latest writings he has come out in favour of measures more far-reaching than anything that has ever been proposed by Harold Lasswell and his colleagues. Skinner says that the only way to build a better life for men is to undertake a wholesale reconstruction of the environment, since it is, he believes, the environment which determines everybody's state of mind. Skinner, in other words, has come out frankly in favour of what Sir Karl Popper used to call 'utopian social engineering'. Many people share Skinner's belief. But what nobody could possibly argue is that a behaviourism which is directed towards the improvement of men through the reconstruction of the environment is a science concerned with the realm of fact alone. When Skinner speaks of 'improvement' and 'better cultures' and a 'better way of life' he betrays himself as someone who is talking of norms.[1] If his positivism is not therapeutic, that is only because it is more radically programmatic. The dogma of the divorce between fact and value has never been repudiated. But the writings of those who subscribe to it serve themselves to refute it.

There is no politics in heaven because everybody is perfectly good and perfectly wise. There is politics on earth because men have partial but not a perfect moral insight and a partial but not a perfect understanding.[2] Politics is in part an argument about values between men who agree about some values but disagree about others. If they did not agree about some – about the desirability of truth and justice, for example – they could not engage in a dialogue at all; there could be no politics. But the dialogue is unending because there is no perfect knowledge of justice, and every man has to subscribe to his own order of axiological preferences.

Politics is, secondly, an argument about the future, or more narrowly, about the future consequences of proposed lines of action. Again, no man knows the future. We must each make our own conjecture or surmise, and justify that surmise as best we can. A politician must argue: if we do this, and so and so will come about: and then go on to make a value judgement once again and say, that this so-and-so which would come about would be good or bad. In talking politics we cannot avoid making value judgements. They are

1. In *The Listener*, 30 September 1971, Skinner writes (p. 431): 'Governments still hold the individual responsible and are said to be best if they govern least because the individual is then free to behave well because of inner virtues. All this continues to direct attention from the task of building a social environment in which people behave well . . . and lead enjoyable lives. It obscures the fact that the problem is to design better cultures – not better people.' See also B. F. Skinner *Beyond Freedom and Dignity*; New York, Knopf, 1971; London, Cape, 1972.

2. For an enlargement on this point see J. R. Lucas, *The Principles of Politics*, Oxford University Press, 1966, sections 1 and 2.

part of the very words in use. Besides, the most serious form of political speech is an argument, and an argument entails an appeal to norms of more than one kind. The most absorbing political arguments are those which embody both disagreements about the moral aspects of a projected policy and disagreements about the probable future consequences of adopting it.

I speak of 'moral aspects', but it is worth noticing that there are at least three types of value judgement which rest on a concept of right or good. First, there are considerations of duty in the strict sense of the word. If there is any universal moral law at all, it is the rule that contracts must be kept. Locke once said that the keeping of promises was a duty that belonged to man as man and not only as a member of civil society. If men are bound to keep promises, then it seems not unreasonable to argue that institutions, including states, are similarly bound. Secondly, there are considerations of prudence, by which I mean the use of intelligent foresight to avert future harm. Again, it is commonly held that a government ought to protect its people from injury. *Salus populi suprema est lex*. Thirdly, there is a further type of value judgement which is made in political arguments: and this of the good conceived in terms of public advantage or gain. Prudence is negative: it is a matter of avoiding evil, or preventing things getting worse than they are. Gain, or what is often called utility, is a matter of promoting what is expected to be an improvement.

Other values, such as liberty and compassion, are invoked in the course of political arguments, but these three kinds occupy a central place; and indeed even liberty is often expressed as a right, one of the historic rights of man. The notion of right is logically connected with that of duty and each is a different aspect of the concept of justice. It would hardly be an exaggeration to say that almost all political arguments, by their very nature, turn on considerations of justice or prudence or public gain. Some politicians are often suspected of being the spokesmen of private or sectional interests; and conceivably some of them are. But they must hide that fact. The important thing is that nobody in a political argument can stand up and say 'My friends or clients *want* this or that'. Admittedly in business negotiations and the like the representative of one party can say: 'Our price is such and we won't take less'. His strength is that negotiation will depend entirely on his power to enforce his demands, and has nothing to do with the justice of his claim. But negotiation is not politics, and politics is not negotiation. In politics you must appeal to justice or the public interest. A politician who pleads for better pensions for wounded soldiers cannot simply say: 'These men want more, and won't take less.' He must argue that they are entitled to more: that it is just for them to have it. In other words, he must translate the claim into a right. In another case, a political speaker will appeal to prudence. We hear a lot of this in debates about defence and finance. If someone in Parliament wants to recommend a rather mean policy, such as withdrawing the subsidy on the fees of overseas students or taking away the free milk from schoolchildren, he cannot simply stand up and say: foreign students and schoolchildren have no vote so let's make them suffer first; he has to get up and say: these measures are extravagant; and prudence compels us to cut down on luxuries. Then, of course, the argument becomes, what is and what is not a luxury, a waste to be eliminated in the interests of economy. In addition to such appeals to prudence, there is the appeal to public gain or utility. A politician advocating the building of an airport would be a fool to say: 'The shareholders in the aviation industry desire this innovation.' He will have to argue that increased facilities for travel and trade would be to the public advantage. He must depict the proposed innovation as an improvement from the point of view of all.

One cannot simply give voice to mere demands in politics: one must express claims as just entitlements: one must recommend policies as prudential or advantageous to the public as a whole. One may equally, of course, appeal to the public interest or to some other universal norm. Sometimes such appeals are bogus, or fraudulent; but like all forms of counterfeit, these are entirely dependent on the secure existence of the genuine. However, it is one thing to say that norms are inseparable from politics, and quite another to decide what order of priority should be given to such values in judging a question of public policy. In the case of a private person, it might be readily agreed that duty should come first, prudence second, and considerations of gain last. But we are unlikely to agree that the same hierarchy obtains in people's judgements of proposed political policies. And those who say that Machiavelli was Satan on earth are usually the first to say that, in practical politics, considerations of duty must come second or third to considerations of prudence or gain.

And assuredly the situation of the private person, thinking of his own duties and desires *is* different from the situation of the statesman thinking of what to do on behalf of his country. It is by no means clear what is meant by an institutional obligation, for although it is explained by analogy with a private person's obligation, it is clearly different. For the man who is obliged is the same man as he who promises. But in the case of a state, one ruler or government may give the promise, and another be called upon to keep it. Then again it is one thing for a private person to risk his own neck in the course of duty; but another thing for a statesman to put the lives of all his people in danger. The one might well be heroic: the other could easily be unpardonable folly. Again we should admire the man who decided to forgo all thought of gain for himself. But we might think ill of the statesman who threw away the possibility of gain for his whole people.

So the situation of the statesman is more awkward than that of the private man. Moral dilemmas are fairly rare in private life: but in politics the path of duty is often opposed to what looks like the path of gain, and not infrequently different from the way of prudence. Saint-Simon, I think, once said: '*La politique et la morale ne font jamais bon ménage.*' I do not think this is true, but we can understand why it should be said.

Prudence is unlike duty. We derive our knowledge of our duty from our past promises and our present situation or from our conscience, but prudence entails an estimate of future possibilities. The prudential course of action is one dictated by what a reasonable mind must expect to happen. It is not always easy to be prudent, but it does not demand any superhuman skill. The pursuit of positive gain or improvement is much more difficult. How are we to know that things will turn out one way rather than another, and judge that the long term results will be good rather than bad? In the advanced industrial societies of the West nature has been ravaged by people who thought that what they were doing was improving life for themselves and their posterity. To sense future danger and avoid it is sometimes more or less instinctive, but to envisage the unfolding of a future good calls for a more uncommon wisdom. In politics men need, as Machiavelli tells us, a very profound worldliness: an experience of life and affairs, and a culture of the mind which teaches men what they may expect other men to do. They can never *know*; but they can learn to measure probabilities. Measure them, of course, only to a limited extent, for in politics, as Machiavelli again reminds us, a prominent part is always played by *fortuna* or luck.

In recent times, we have had the promise of a more comprehensive and systematic futurology. Part of the programme of positivist social science was to discover laws which would apply to the future as well as to the past and present. There is an idea going back as far as Francis Bacon that science will save us, and the behavioural sciences have been infected with the same conception of their mission. They promise to save us by enabling the statesman to contemplate future problems in the light of calculated projections from accumulated facts and solve such problems with the aid of carefully formulated laws of human behaviour. And how often do we see our behaviouralists, waiting in the wings of the theatre of politics, a large stack of data in one hand and a begging bowl in the other: 'Give us the money for research', they say, 'and we will give you the solutions.' This is what is promised. But what the politician gets is information. Rivers of it. There is indeed so much information pouring forth today that politicians and public servants are flooded with it. Information has become a real threat to knowledge. The more information you have the more you need an interpreter, an expert. But can such experts be trusted? If behavioural science could really be value-free, its practitioners might readily seem to be, almost by definition, impartial. But when behavioural science turns out to be impregnated with admitted or unadmitted value judgements, suspicions are aroused. Politicians have indeed become increasingly suspicious. The tendency nowadays is for the statesman to look for expert advice only to experts whose political, or ideological persuasions are akin to his own: we read in recent British political

2

memoirs that Mr Crosland, as Minister of Education, set up his own informal 'brains trust' on educational reform composed of Labour Party intellectuals. And on a larger scale, when President Kennedy and President Nixon each called in professors from Harvard to advise him in Washington, Mr Kennedy chose progressives and Mr Nixon chose conservatives. Although their choices often worked out well, this is an unfortunate development. It is also reactionary: a reaction, notably, against faith in a *wertfrei* social science and towards ideological social theory, towards the attitude which says: 'Everybody is ideologically biased, so let me have someone who is biased in my way.' This reactionary argument rests on the assumption, which I believe to be false, that you have either to make no value judgements at all, or make ideologically slanted ones, that there is no middle way between being *wertfrei* and being biased. The truth of the matter, I think, is much simpler. And that is, that we must each make our own preferences but that we ought to be able to justify our preferences. Reasonable grounds can be given for some evaluations that cannot be given for others. There is a very great difference between a measured and critical recognition of values, and the rigid adhesion to a doctrine or a prejudice. 'Criticism' is a crucial word. For in the theatre of politics, the political philosopher is a kind of dramatic critic. He may grow fretful in the stalls and yearn to mount the stage himself, but just as critics are notoriously bad actors, so philosophers make wretched politicians. We may think of Gentile becoming Mussolini's minister of education, or Heidegger joining the Nazi party, or Lukács going to Moscow to support Stalin. Or perhaps it is better not to think of them.

Then again there is a temptation for the philosopher to see himself as a dramatist, writing the plays which the politicians perform. Lenin sometimes fancied himself as enacting a drama which had been composed by Marx, but, if he did, he altered the script so much that Marx would not have recognized it. And in truth, of course, Lenin was both playwright and player. Rightly so. For in the theatre of politics there is no place for any other kind of dramatist. The politician is an actor who must furnish his own dialogue, even if he does not actually write it. That is why we judge him by his words. Rousseau was right when he said that the orator is no one but himself. In politics the orator can never rid himself of responsibility for what he says.

The critic is there to remind him of it. He is there also to analyse and explain the drama, and to appraise the performances. Without dramatic criticism, dramatic art would probably decline. Without political philosophy politics might well go on as merrily as ever. The only trouble is that it would not be understood, it would be a practice without consciousness of the norms which inform its activity, ignorant even of its own identity or nature. It is now some years since Mr Peter Laslett uttered his notorious remark that 'for the moment, anyway, political philosophy is dead.'[1] Mr Laslett may not have meant those words to be taken altogether seriously since he wrote them in an introduction to a series of essays in political philosophy.[2] But if the day ever comes when political philosophy is really dead, the triumph of information over knowledge will be complete.

1. See his introduction to *Philosophy, Politics and Society*, vol. I, Oxford, Blackwell, 1956.

2. In his introduction to vol. II of this same series, dated 1962, Mr Laslett detected a 'revival' of political philosophy.

Some Aspects
of the History of
Freedom

The word 'freedom' has two characteristics which ought not to be overlooked. The first is that it is incompletely descriptive: to be told that someone is free is to be told something that is less than fully intelligible. Is he free from captivity, from debt, from social engagements, from duties, from the marriage tie? The possibilities are innumerable. There are so many different situations, and different kinds of situation, which can 'bind' a man. Thus we need to know of a man who is said to be free, what he is free from, or, alternatively, what he is free to do: that he is free to emigrate, for example, or to marry or to dispose of certain property or to accept a social invitation. In any case we need more knowledge.

The second important feature of the word 'freedom' is that it implies liking, approval, some form of favourable attitude towards the situation mentioned. In the jargon of philosophy it is a 'laudatory' word, a 'normative word' that 'confers value', it is what Gilbert Ryle used to call 'a hurrah word'. Freedom is, by definition, a good thing. A prisoner who is pleased to be released, a soldier who is happy to be demobilized, a wife who is glad to be divorced: all such people are likely to use the word 'freedom'. But someone who passes from a condition which pleases him to one which displeases him, who passes, for example, from a good job to the bread line of the unemployed, from a happy marriage to a miserable widowerhood, from a luxury liner to an open raft, will not say he is 'free'. This is because he does not feel he has gained anything; he has lost something.

The word 'freedom' signifies in its most general use, the absence of constraints, burdens, frustrations; and it is because we do not, on the whole, like constraints, burdens and frustrations that we use this smiling word 'freedom' to signify their absence. If something is absent that we should like to have present, we do not speak of being free, we use some other word such as 'lacking' or 'missing' or 'wanting'. We read about 'tax-free investments'; but who has ever heard of a 'dividend-free investment'? If we are without a certain skill, we usually regret it. I would say: 'I lack Spanish', not 'I am free from Spanish'. Again, I would say: 'The spare wheel is missing from my car', not 'My car is free from spare wheels'. We should not be surprised to hear someone say that his house was 'free of rats', but we should be surprised to hear him say that his house 'lacked rats'. This is not to suggest that everyone would use the same word in the same circumstances. Different people have different feelings in similar circumstances; and only the man who knows the feelings knows what is the right word to express those feelings.

Freedom is the absence of constraint; but it needs to be added that not all constraints are unwelcome. There is an element of constraint in every rule, and we certainly do not find all rules irksome. We need rules, and more often than not we want them. Promises and contracts 'bind' us morally, and although there is an antithesis between freedom and bondage, we do not regard all our duties as disagreeable. As David Hume said, most men are usually happy to do their duty. This is one reason why it sounds paradoxical to speak of an antithesis between duty and freedom, even though our duties 'bind' us. Besides, we are 'bound' only in a metaphorical sense. In more literal language we are obliged. And only a free being can have an obligation. The concept of duty is inseparable from that of freedom.

There is a connexion also between law and freedom. Men desire a system of law; and indeed we have a word which denotes a condition of undesirable lawlessness, 'licence'. This word 'licence' carries with it an element of condemnation which corresponds to the element of praise in the word 'freedom' – or in the word 'liberty', which is its synonym. Naturally, people often disagree about the desirability of certain specific laws or rules, and one person will use the word 'freedom' where another would use the word 'licence'. Consider the example of the progressive school which was run in the

1920s by Bertrand and Dora Russell. There were none of the usual school rules about work and conduct. The Russells said proudly: 'This is a school where freedom prevails.' But other people, people who did not share the Russells' views on education, used to say, disapprovingly: 'This is a school where licence prevails.' The facts were not in dispute. The witnesses simply disagreed in their judgement of those facts; and each person's judgement dictated his choice of language.

There is a famous remark of Thomas Hobbes about the liberty of subjects being the silence of the law, and, in a sense, there is no denying the truth of it. If there is no law forbidding public meetings, no law controlling the press, no law forbidding the sale of liquor, then in all these cases the silence of the law might easily be read as the measure of the liberty of the subjects. But if there is no law against murder, robbery or assault, no law to protect rights of any kind, then the silence of the law will not so readily be taken as the measure of the people's freedom. Such a thought is elaborated in one of Locke's arguments, which can be read as a reply to Hobbes even though it may not have been written as such, namely Locke's argument that law enlarges liberty. In paragraph 57 of his *Second Treatise of Government*, Locke says:

For law, in its true notion is not so much the limitation as the direction of a free and intelligent agent to his proper interest, and prescribes no further than is for the general good of those under that Law. Could they be happier without it, the Law, as a useless thing, would of itself vanish; and that ill deserves the name of confinement which hedges us in only from bogs and precipices. So that however it may be mistaken, the end of law is not to abolish or restrain, but to preserve and enlarge freedom. For in all the states of created beings capable of laws, where there is no law, there is no freedom. For liberty is to be free from restraint and violence from others, which cannot be where there is no law; but freedom is not, as we are told, a liberty for every man to do what he lists (for who could be free, when every other man's humour might domineer over him?), but a liberty to dispose and order as he lists, his person, actions, possessions, and his whole property, with the allowance of those laws under which he is, and therein not to be subject to the arbitrary will of another, but freely follow his own.

The disagreement between Hobbes and Locke could perhaps be summed up by saying that Hobbes dispenses with the word 'licence'. For him political freedom is never more than a residual freedom. In the state of nature, which is a condition of total anarchy, there is complete freedom. In political societies, there is only a limited number of civil liberties, although some political societies provide more than others. Hobbes does not seem to have had any strong feelings about the extent of the civil liberties which any one system afforded; he was more concerned to press his point that any civil society is preferable to anarchy. But Locke distinguishes between three conditions: the state of nature, which is lawless in the sense that it is without positive law; a constitutional state, which has both liberty and law; and a despotism, which has bad laws and no liberty. Thus Locke understands freedom as something distinct from both the licence of anarchy and the oppression of despotic rule, whereas Hobbes understands freedom as that which is opposed to the constraints of government as such.

I will call these two conceptions of freedom the Lockean and the Hobbesian, although they are certainly not held by those two philosophers alone. Each has its own theoretical and practical implications. Hobbesian freedom exists in the full sense only where there is no government. There will be miscellaneous civil liberties in any and every state, but Hobbes does not permit any contrast between a free society and despotism. No civil society is free, although some have more liberties than others. There is thus no sense in which the Hobbesian could fight a war for freedom or engage in a revolution for the sake of freedom – except perhaps in the case of an anarchist, who might launch a revolution with the aim of overthrowing governments altogether. It is ironical that Hobbes, who was such an authoritarian and who dreaded anarchy above all things, should have formulated better than many anarchists the anarchist conception of freedom as that which stands opposed to government, the conception of liberty as the silence of the law. At the level of practical politics, there thus seem to be two lines open to the exponent of Hobbesian freedom: either a quietistic and grateful acceptance of any established government no matter how despotic (which was Hobbes's own line, and logically his line, since he thought that anarchy was the worst of evils), or alternatively, an attitude of hostility to any government on the ground that all government is opposed to freedom (this is the anarchist choice; making the same Hobbesian identification of freedom with anarchy, he, for the sake of freedom, chooses anarchy).

The Lockean conception of freedom has other implications and raises other problems. First, there is the problem of distinguishing between the licence of anarchy and the freedom of the rule of law under a constitutional system. Then there is the problem of distinguishing between such a good system of law and the 'bad law' of a despotism which Locke thinks may be even more inimical to freedom than is the licence of anarchy. Furthermore, there is the practical problem for those who understand freedom in this Lockean sense, of setting up and maintaining a civil order which is neither anarchic on the one hand nor despotic on the other.

There is a distinction elaborated by Sir Isaiah Berlin in his lecture on 'Two Concepts of Liberty'[1] which might be introduced at this point: the distinction between 'positive' and 'negative' freedom. It might well be suggested that the Hobbesian notion is one of negative freedom – freedom from any political or legal constraints – whereas the Lockean notion is one of positive freedom – a measured, limited, lawful freedom expressed in the language of rights. But I think this might be misleading. For although the Lockean conception was developed into something distinctly 'positive' by later theorists such as Hegel, Locke himself adhered to a 'negative' formulation. In the paragraph ahead, quoted from his *Second Treatise*, Locke says that 'liberty is to be free from restraint and violence from others'. Law is needed (he suggests) to ensure freedom from the kind of restraint and violence which exists in the state of nature, but this does not mean that *any* kind of law is conducive to freedom; and indeed Locke says that the sort of law which is upheld by despotic rulers is inimical to freedom. Only a certain kind of law preserves and enlarges men's liberty. So Lockean freedom is defined 'negatively' even though it is tied to a conception of law which is understood 'positively' as 'the direction of a free and intelligent agent to his proper interest'. Locke takes care to add that this law 'prescribes no

1. Reproduced in *Four Essays on Liberty*, Oxford University Press, 1969.

2*

further than is for the general good of those under the law'. Liberty for Locke in this sense is the 'silence of *superfluous* laws'.

This emphasis of Locke's on the connexion between liberty and law naturally calls to mind the old Latin tag: *Libertas est potestas faciendi quod jure liceat.* And it may prompt us to wonder whether the Romans had a distinctive conception of freedom. What did they understand by the word *'libertas'*? The evidence we have suggests that it meant different things to them at different phases in their history.[1] One of the circumstances which helped to shape the idea of *libertas* for Roman minds was the existence of slavery. In the first place, a free man was simply a man who was not a slave. An important moment in Roman history occurred when, in Wirszubski's words, the relationship between the king and the people came to be 'considered to be analogous to the relation between master and slave'. For this reason, *libertas* in its first and most elementary political sense meant freedom from kingly oppression. At this stage of Roman history, the concept of freedom which men held was an unambiguous one: freedom stood opposed to monarchy conceived as mastery. With the establishment of the Republic, the word *libertas* acquired a different resonance. It ceased to have such a limited and specific use. It took on more than one meaning. In the first place, the notion of liberty came to be connected with the republican form of government as such. In Wirszubski's words: 'The Romans dated their own freedom from the abolition of the monarchy, and identified with this the republican form of constitution.'[2] This is understandable enough; for if freedom simply means the absence of monarchical dominion, a constitution which eliminates monarchy introduces freedom. To attain freedom in this sense, all that is required is a republic. But once the Romans secured their republic, they began to think of freedom as something more than the mere absence of kingly oppression. They began to think of it as being composed of the basic rights of citizenship. They did

1. In this connexion see especially C. Wirszubski's *Libertas as a Political Idea at Rome during the late Republic and Early Principate*, Cambridge University Press, 1950.
2. Ibid., p. 5.

not use the word *libertas* to name the whole range of positive civil rights, because these were not evenly distributed, some citizens obviously enjoying a larger share of them than others; but the central and indispensable rights which any man had to have in order to be a citizen at all were understood as constituting freedom or *libertas*.

Undoubtedly *libertas* became a word of marked rhetorical potency. Certain political factions made it their motto: those who asserted their devotion to the republican constitution proclaimed their devotion to *libertas*. And outside Rome, the people who demanded *libertas*, the Allies, for example, and the Latins, were clearly understood to be thinking of citizenship. In asking for *libertas* they were asking for civil rights. In both senses, this Roman conception of freedom can be distinguished from democratic conceptions, whether those of ancient Greek or of the modern world. For the Romans, to be free meant having a vote in choosing a ruler; it did not mean ruling oneself. Cicero, for example, spoke of a properly balanced constitution as one in which the magistrate has enough power, the Senate enough authority, and the people enough freedom, but Cicero was not thinking, in Hobbesian terms, that the less power the magistrate had then the more freedom the people would have; still less did he see any conflict or competition between freedom and authority.

It is not difficult to see why the Romans stressed the connexion between liberty and law. For whether *libertas* is identified with the republican constitution or identified with the enjoyment of civil rights, it is indebted to a conception of law for its very meaning. Besides, the Romans distinguished *libertas* from *licentia* even more forcefully than we distinguish liberty from licence; *licentia* meant lawlessness in the most literal sense. It is interesting to notice that when the Roman republic was transformed into a principate, the idea of *libertas* underwent a further modification. Many historians say that the Roman republic disappeared because the people became less devoted to what they had regarded as freedom, and began to yearn for peace and security even at the expense of liberty. Moreover we can detect in the literature of this period of autocracy, evidence of newer and non-political theories of freedom gaining currency in Rome. For example, it became fashionable in certain quarters to think that inner freedom is more important than civil freedom. At the same time, we find several polemical writers suggesting that liberty is not only dependent on the law but is identical with the law, and hence that the more the law is asserted by a powerful ruler, the more is freedom upheld.

If Roman *libertas* was indeed inseparable from the Roman republic, then it is hardly surprising that that kind of freedom at any rate disappeared when the republic disappeared. Conceivably Caesar was right to think that the old Roman constitution was appropriate only to a city state and that for a universal empire, a different kind of constitution was needed – one with a single ruler at its head. At all events, Caesar was victorious; and the republic came to an end. Cato's suicide seems a logical act: he preferred to die while he was still a free man, rather than live in what he under-stood as servitude. In the words of Seneca: 'By divine law they were indissolubly united. Neither did Cato survive freedom nor freedom survive Cato.' But of course the emperors tried to exploit the prestige of the word *libertas* to their advantage. Augustus called himself the liberator: *vindex libertatis*, as we read on his coins. But all he could fairly claim to have done was to have freed the community from the particular oppression which held sway before his own. Later emperors made the same sort of claim.[1] But, as Max Pohlenz writes:

It only meant that they had destroyed one ruler to put themselves in his place. . . . People quickly grew accustomed to the new situation and the opposition fell silent. . . . In the capital after their loss of liberty, the great majority were satisfied with bread and circuses. In the provinces, the people were quite content and glad that law and order now prevailed. Above all they enjoyed gratefully a boon the world had hardly known before . . . peace.

With the decline of political freedom, the time was ripe for more sophisticated and metaphysical notions of freedom to come into favour. But Roman thought did not originate such ideas; they were borrowed from Greek and oriental sources. And here the temptation

1. Max Pohlenz, *Griechische Freiheit*, Heidelberg, Quelle & Meyer, 1960; trans. into English as *Freedom in Greek Life and Thought*, Dordrecht, D. Reidel, 1966.

to look at Greek conceptions of freedom is irresistible. It is a commonplace that the idea of political liberty did not have anything like the prominence in ancient Greece that it had in Rome. The Greek political philosophers were more interested in justice, and their emphasis reflected something that was fairly general. Even so, we do often find the word ἐλευθερία (*eleutheria*) being used to mean political liberty; and once again we may notice that the word is used rather differently at different times and places.

The scholarly literature on this subject is exiguous; but two fairly up-to-date books in German deal with it at some length: Max Pohlenz's *Griechische Freiheit*, already cited and the first two hundred pages of Alexander Rüstow's *Weg der Freiheit*.[1] Rüstow treats freedom as political freedom only, but Pohlenz gives attention equally to the various philosophical concepts of freedom that are put forward by Greek thinkers. Many of these thinkers are critical, and even scornful, of freedom conceived as political freedom. In the few essays that have been written in English on the Greek idea of ἐλευθερία we find some bewildering remarks. For example, in a well-known paper by Hannah Arendt entitled 'Freedom and Politics' the suggestion is made that 'in the classical era freedom was regarded exclusively and radically as a political concept' and that 'freedom in the philosophical sense was introduced into philosophy much later by St Augustine'.[2] Mrs Arendt is surely wrong in thinking this, for the Greeks entertained a variety of non-political notions of freedom. J. L. Myers, in his *Political Ideas of the Greeks* gives as *the* Greek conception of freedom something which is scarcely political at all: the Greeks, he says, understood freedom as 'self mastery' or 'being grown up'.[3]

Undoubtedly what Myers speaks of is *one* Greek conception, but manifestly it is not the only one. We cannot even speak of a single Greek notion of *political* freedom. For as in Rome, that notion changed with changing times. The earliest form in which political

---

1. This is vol. II of Rüstow's *Ortbestimmung der Gegenwart*, Zürich, Erlenbach, 1952.

2. Mrs Arendt's paper is published in A. Hunold, ed., *Freedom and Serfdom*, Dordrecht, Reidel, 1961.

3. J. L. Myers, *The Political Ideas of the Greeks*, London, Edward Arnold, 1935, pp. vi and 196.

freedom was talked about in ancient Greece seems to have been simply the freedom of Greeks from alien, and specifically, from Persian rule. This is still a very familiar sense of political freedom, the one we have in mind when we speak of the freedom of the Poles or the Czechs. 'National freedom' is the expression that would be used nowadays. We can hardly apply the word 'nation' to the ancient Greeks, because it would be an anachronism, but we may allow ourselves to speak of the freedom of the Greek people. Herodotus in his history depicts the Greek war against the Persians as one of liberation: again an arrestingly modern conception. In Athens the people put up a statue and a temple to Zeus Eleutherios – Zeus the Liberator – which affords another example of the use of the word 'freedom' to mean Greek liberation. However, if freedom means freedom from alien rule, much depends on what is meant by 'alien rule'. And after the Persians had been expelled, some Greeks who lived elsewhere than in Athens felt that the supremacy of Athens in the Greek confederation was itself a form of 'alien rule'. Thus we find the word 'freedom' being used at this period to mean local freedom or autonomy. Indeed it is this way of thinking which authorized Sparta, which few people would now consider the ideal model of a free society, to go into battle against Athens with the cry 'Freedom for the Greeks!', meaning, of course, 'Independence for small cities'.

In Athens itself a more elaborate notion of political freedom developed with democratic government. Pericles in his famous Funeral Oration gives a very exalted and idealized account of it. He claims that the men of Athens live as they choose, but that, being patriotic men, they put the interest of the city before their personal concerns. Their aim, says Pericles, is the free development of the human personality, understood as that of a citizen; and a citizen is a man who gives willing assent to the laws he has helped to institute. Plato provides a very different picture of Athenian freedom.[1] He uses the same word ἐλευθερια and he agrees that the democratic man makes freedom his aim. But freedom, says Plato, is understood as 'men doing what they want to do'. Not, as Pericles claims, doing what they want to do but wanting what is good and being uncon-

1. *The Republic*, viii, 557 B, 'On the Democratic Man'.

strained in putting their country first and obeying the law. Far from it: Plato depicts men who do what they want to do as men who live selfishly and obey only their own desires. This is not to say that Plato always uses the word ἐλευθερια in a pejorative way. Indeed the first reference to it in *The Republic* (which occurs in paragraph 329 D) clearly implies that freedom is a good thing: we hear Cephalus saying that old age has given him peace and freedom because he is no longer troubled by sexual desire. This is a sense of the word freedom which is to recur in Greek (and other) philosophers: freedom understood as freedom from the inner constraints of passion.

Aristotle in at least one famous passage in the *Politics* (Book V. ix. 15, 16) echoes Plato's feeling that there is something mean about the conception of freedom as 'doing what one likes, each man living for any end he chances to desire'. Like Plato, Aristotle connects this conception of freedom with the democratic ethos. And again like Plato, Aristotle uses the word ἐλευθερια in different senses elsewhere in his writings. Although all questions of Greek etymology tend to be controversial, there are good grounds for thinking that the word ἐλευθερια is rooted in 'to go where one wills' and Epictetus (Book IV.i, 34) explains freedom in this way: 'I go wherever I wish; I come from whence I wish.' Freedom is thus freedom of movement; and this is perhaps the most primitive sense of freedom for the Greek mind. Thus, if we can say of the ancient Greek, as we can of the modern English language, that freedom is opposed to constraint, then we must add that a constraint is felt to be a constraint because it is something which hinders motion towards a chosen end. Pericles praises freedom not only because it entails by definition being unconstrained, but because contingently, the free people of Athens chose *well* (at any rate, Pericles thinks they do). Plato and Aristotle, who do not take the same view of the choices these free people make, who think indeed that these people use their freedom to make bad choices, attack this type of freedom, which they speak of as *democratic* freedom. They prepare the way for the suggestion that there may be other and better types of freedom.

This suggestion is developed by a number of Greek philosophers, and their various conceptions of inner freedom, moral freedom and

metaphysical freedom compete with the older ideas of political freedom, whether collective or individual. Some of the philosophical
notions of freedom are frankly antipolitical. Aristippus, for example,
puts forward the suggestion that to be free is to be independent of
external things, and Diogenes carries the idea even further: freedom
for him is complete non-attachment. Others writers develop the idea
that Plato puts into the mouth of Cephalus that the most important
freedom for man is freedom from the flesh and its lusts. And later we
meet the Stoic conception of freedom, which brings it back into
politics though not into the *polis*, by making freedom at once a distinguishing characteristic of reasoning beings and a universal right
which such beings possess. It ought not to surprise us that the
Greeks had so many different notions of freedom, since we ourselves
have no fewer. But there is one conception of freedom which the
ancient Greeks seem not to have had at all: and that is freedom in the
sense of the freedom of the will. This is a concept which we can
fairly date from St Augustine; and if Mrs Arendt had said, not that
the philosophical concept of freedom dated from St Augustine, but
that the concept of free will did, then her suggestion would be readily
accepted.

But let us leap from the ancient to the modern world. In England in
the sixteenth and seventeenth centuries, the word 'freedom' was
much on men's lips. And it was used as often as not in a sense of
political freedom. Or rather it was used in at least two distinct
senses of political freedom. The first, and more 'traditional' sense,
we might speak of as chartered freedom. In medieval times, the word
'freedom' suggested to many Englishmen the rights and liberties and
privileges that went with being an Englishman. In a more limited
sense, the word 'freedom' denoted the additional rights that went
with being a burgess, a registered taxpayer or citizen. Here freedom
is plainly connected with rights, and we can perhaps discern an
analogy with ancient Rome, though it is not an analogy one should
press too far. In late medieval England, as in Rome, freedom means
something which all citizens enjoy and also something of which some
citizens enjoy more than others. Hence we find 'freedom' often
spoken of as the special privilege of the gentleman. Chaucer, for

example, says of one of his knights: 'He was of knighthood and free-dom flower.' In Germany freedom at this time is also understood as a mark of privilege: another name for 'Baron' is 'Freiherr'.

The medieval idea of freedom as chartered freedom exists side by side with another notion of political freedom, which Sir Isaiah Berlin might want to call 'negative': this is the notion that to be free is simply not to be dominated by anybody in office. One reason why this notion becomes so prominent in the early modern period is that the rise of absolutism in the sixteenth century had undermined the traditional basis of 'chartered freedom'. But even then it was not entirely new. We find it expressed, for example, in the poetry of William Langland, who was born around 1330. There are some verses of his about liberty which begin:

> Neither King nor knight, constable nor mayor
> Shall overbear the commons, nor summon them to court.

And in a poet born in the fifteenth century, John Skelton, freedom is expressed as something to be defended against the domination of the clergy:

> The poor people they yoke
> With summons and citations
> And excommunications.

Freedom for these poets is clearly understood as the absence of domination by the established powers, whether royal, feudal, ecclesiastical, ministerial or municipal. The Englishman of the Middle Ages had no reason to single out any of these powers as the sole source of constraint; indeed the ordinary man gained a good deal in the way of freedom as a result of the very divisions of power and the rivalries between temporal and spiritual rulers, between kings and noblemen. The English of the Middle Ages had no reason to regard freedom, as the Romans once did, as something directly opposed to monarchy. The English medieval kings were far too limited and circumscribed in their powers to enact the role of the despot.

This may explain why the notion of liberty has never been tied in England, as it was in Rome, to the idea of a republican con-stitution. Assuredly, England became a republic of sorts under

Cromwell after the death of Charles I, but that was a transformation that no one desired. Even Cromwell was a monarchist, with the vision of himself as monarch. The King's enemies in Parliament had wished simply to introduce a reformed monarchy, and it was only because Charles I stubbornly refused to be constitutional monarch, that the Puritan victors in the English Civil War had to set up a republic. A handful of intellectuals, such as Milton, tried to propagate the ideology of republicanism in England, but their efforts were unavailing, and the eleven years of the Puritan Commonwealth were felt to be so disagreeable by most Englishmen that republicanism, which had never been popular, fell into lasting disrepute. The French, like the ancient Romans, were able later to date their freedom from the introduction of republican government; but the English could not, and never were to do so. Hence one notable difference between the traditional English conception of political freedom and that of the French.

Medieval Englishmen often felt that the King was on their side, and hence on the side of freedom against the oppression of bishops and barons; so it is hardly surprising that as many Englishmen were prompted in the seventeenth century to fight for freedom on the side of Charles I as were prompted to fight for freedom on the side of the Parliament. The cry of liberty was perhaps more often heard on the Parliamentary side, but as reflective men of the time observed, this did not mean much. Locke himself noted in his private journal in 1659: 'The popular assertions of public liberty are the greatest engrossers of it too.'[1]

The seventeenth century in England was, of course, a period of great political disturbance. And it is natural that the thinkers of the time should apply their minds to the attempt to rescue the concept of freedom from falling altogether into disrepute. We can, I think, detect at least three notions of freedom in the theoretical literature of the period. There are the two already mentioned; the Hobbesian, according to which freedom is the absence of political constraint, and the Lockean, according to which freedom is the absence of any constraint other than that of a good system of law. The third conception

1. Quoted in M. Cranston: *Locke, a biography*, London, Longman, New York, Macmillan, 1957, p. 59.

of freedom is one which can be found in some of the writings of Milton, where he defines freedom as being unconstrained in acting well.

This 'Miltonic' concept of freedom if we may so call it, although it was not Milton's only way of speaking of freedom, has an important place in the intellectual history of America. In the early Puritan societies of Massachusetts, liberty was conceived of in two ways. In the first place it was understood as freedom from the kind of Anglican orthodoxy which was established in England. In the second place, liberty was understood as the freedom to do only what was right. And indeed in Massachusetts men were often 'forced to be free' in the sense that they were often forced to conform to the Puritan rules of conduct. Naturally some inhabitants of Massachusetts felt that this 'Miltonic' form of freedom was an oppression as bad as that of Anglican England; and indeed a number of those early colonists appealed to the King of England to protect them from their local, or provincial, oppressors. The colony of Rhode Island was founded, under the protection of the British monarch, by people who found the Puritan rule, or 'Miltonic' liberty, of Massachusetts intolerable.

Hence it would be a mistake to think that the American notion of freedom in the seventeenth century was republican. And even in the eighteenth century, when the war of independence was fought and the American republic instituted, there was a marked lack of ideological republicanism in America, and even of what might be termed a republican ethos. The victorious American colonists, like the victorious English Roundheads in the seventeenth century, found themselves in a situation where they had to set up for themselves a nation without a king; and since their whole conception of the nation was that of a kingdom, they faced the paradoxical task of establishing a kingless kingdom. Their republicanism was in this sense profoundly negative. In America there was not, as there had been in ancient Rome, and as there was later to be in France, any identification of liberty with the republican state as such. Far from becoming, in this manner, *étatiste*, the Americans retained their suspicious, hostile attitude to the state even though they had made that state their own.

Professor Carl Friedrich, in *Constitutional Government and Democracy*, suggests an explanation of this. Although George III was the villain of revolutionary polemics, it was the bureaucracy which the American people actually felt and detested, detested because it was both oppressive and inadequate. 'This experience,' Friedrich writes, 'created a permanent suspicion of executive power which has stood in the way of responsible government service ever since.'[1]

It was the absence of any republican ideology in the American revolution which enabled Edmund Burke perfectly logically to commend it while condemning the French Revolution. The American revolution was, in this sense, conservative, or at any rate, Lockean. Historians are sometimes accused of exaggerating the influence of Locke in the American revolution, but the key documents of the period, including the Federalist Papers, are written in an unmistakably Lockean idiom. The makers of the American republic, as Friedrich has pointed out, drew on past, and therefore on British experience.[2]

If we can speak of a distinctly American political attitude emerging at the end of the eighteenth century, then the word we should use to describe it would be 'democratic' rather than republican. Locke himself noticed early in the seventeenth century that there was a tendency towards what he called 'a numerous democracy' in the American colonies because those colonies were socially egalitarian: they had no aristocracy. And Locke who (despite his reputation) disliked democracy, proposed the institution of an aristocracy in Carolina as a means of correcting this trend towards democracy. Of course Locke's advice was not taken, so that an egalitarian, and in time a democratic society produced, as he expected it to produce, a democratic constitution.

Even so, the constitution that was thus democratized was a Lockean one. America never modelled herself on the one country

1. Carl J. Friedrich, *Constitutional Government and Democracy*, Boston, Ginn, 1950, pp. 42–3.
2. 'The rich experience of British administrative genius had already been at work in creating the framework of a government service into which the constitutionalizing forces merely had to put new men to carry on', *Constitutional Government and Democracy*, p. 43.

which provided an example of democracy in the modern world, Switzerland. For the citizen-soldiers of the sluggish Swiss cantons were deeply *étatiste*, and afforded no model for the rugged individualist of the New World who carried a gun only for his own protection. If the American was prompted to discard the Lockean conception of freedom, it was increasingly in favour of the Hobbesian conception of freedom as freedom from any kind of political dominion. And when the Miltonic conception of liberty declined with the decline of the Puritan rule in Massachusetts, 'American freedom', or the American way of thinking about freedom, whether in politics or other spheres, proved surprisingly often to mean the 'silence of the law', and still does today in Spockian theories of upbringing, for example, or in fashionable American progressive theories of academic organization.

The French have held rather different views of liberty. It was fashionable in France in the eighteenth century to speak of England as the 'mirror of liberty', but it is doubtful whether the French really wanted to adopt the English form of political freedom or whether indeed they really understood what English freedom was. Montesquieu perhaps, for all his mistakes, came closer to it than most; but Montesquieu, as Voltaire noticed, had a vested interest in remodelling France on the English model, because the English constitution, with its House of Lords, gave special privileges to provincial aristocrats like Montesquieu himself in addition to any liberties it bestowed on the common man. Voltaire, who had no reason to love the aristocracy, considered such privileges to be wholly inimical to freedom. Political freedom, as Voltaire understood it, meant freedom above all from the constraints that emanated from the feudal power; and to put down that feudal power, Voltaire was more than willing to elevate the royal power. Voltaire saw feudal power as linked with ecclesiastical power; and it was because he regarded these two sources of constraint, the nobility and the Church, as the greatest enemies of freedom in France, that he saw nothing illogical in favouring at the same time freedom and *le despotisme éclairé*, this latter being understood as an enlarged and enlightened monarchy. This preference was closer to the thinking of

Francis Bacon than to that of Locke and of English or American people generally. Although Bacon's politics found little favour in his own country, the Baconian idea of *le despotisme éclairé*, propagated by Voltaire and the other Encyclopaedists, has had numerous adherents in France and other continental countries, and even a few exponents of it.

Edmund Burke once contrasted the English notion of the rights of Englishmen, which he thought both intelligible and admirable, with the French conception of the rights of man, which he thought absurd. One can understand Burke's point: but he betrays a certain obtuseness. The French had to talk at this abstract level because they had no traditional experience of rights to draw on. Their understanding of liberty was necessarily bookish. On the other hand the French had undoubtedly a concrete knowledge of what stood opposed to freedom: the Church, for example, and all the arbitrary laws and feudal privileges that were characteristic of the *ancien régime*. When Voltaire cried: '*Ecrasez l'infame*' he did not have to explain what *l'infame* was; everybody knew or could readily imagine. Moreover, abstract ways of thinking came easily to the French, just as pragmatic or empirical ways of thinking were becoming habitual in the English-speaking world. French culture, thanks to the endeavours of its Jesuit and Jansenist professors, of its Cartesian philosophers and of its innumerable lawyers, bred rationalists everywhere, so that *liberté* conceived as one of the abstract rights of man was wholly congenial to the French type of mind.

In the French *Declaration of the Rights of Man and the Citizen* liberty is defined as 'being unrestrained in doing anything that does not interfere with the liberty of another', a phrase which puts one in mind of Locke. But the French Revolution was very far from being a movement to enthrone the minimal state and to let the people be; it was very unlike the Glorious Revolution of 1688 which Locke admired so much. Besides, the call for *liberté* was heard at the same time as the cry of *égalité* and *fraternité*, the purge of the aristocracy, the attack on Christianity, the seizure of property and all sorts of other progressive enterprises which were quite incompatible with Locke's kind of liberty, though several of them were foreshadowed by Voltaire and Holbach and the Encyclopaedists generally. But that was the paradoxical manner of the Enlightenment philosophers – demanding liberty from the constraints of the *ancien régime* at one moment and drawing up blue-prints for new forms of despotism at the next. Unfortunately, although it may be possible to believe in liberty and despotism at the same time, it is scarcely possible to have any more than the most parsimonious Hobbesian series of civil liberties under the best of despots.

However, when neo-Roman and Rousseauesque yearnings for republicanism took possession of the French soul, the temptation to identify liberty with the republican form of government was well-nigh inescapable. The republican ideology enables its adherents to believe at the same time in freedom and a strong state. And indeed the republican argument for a strong state is beautifully simple: if the state is the people's state, the people's freedom cannot be diminished if their state is powerful; on the contrary, if their state is enlarged, their freedom is correspondingly increased. But even though this French republican idea of freedom is *étatiste*, it remains essentially individualist. Freedom is still conceived as the possession of each man and each citizen. This is no longer true of the concept of freedom upheld by the nationalist movements in other parts of the world in the nineteenth and twentieth centuries, which transform freedom into a right belonging to *a* people or *a* nation. Freedom is demanded no longer for the man and the citizen, but for Germany or Italy or Nigeria.

And so we seem to have come full circle. The earliest conception of freedom that we can trace in European political thought is that of the Greek people, considered as a people, a freedom contrasted with alien dominion. The same notion is the most widespread of any conception of freedom in the world today. It is perhaps surprising that such an ancient idea of freedom should capture the minds of men in a world as sophisticated as our own. It certainly did not satisfy the Greeks for long. Once they had acquired freedom from foreign oppression, new and more far-reaching forms of liberty were demanded for men and citizens. The mere absence of Persian dominion was the beginning of their experience of freedom, it was not its final consummation. In our own day, 'national' freedom is the often only kind of freedom that the people enjoy. In much of what we call the Third World, freedom from alien rule has become a subject of continuous excitement long after it has been acquired, perhaps because the people there have no other kind of freedom to be grateful for. If the nation has been liberated, the individual is still subject to numerous forms of domination. The old imperial administrator has gone, but only to make way in many places for an indigenous despot.

But if national freedom can thus prove an inadequate acquisition, it is something which many people in the later decades of the twentieth century are still denied. Czechs and Poles, Estonians and Latvians are less fortunate than the inhabitants of the sovereign republics of Senegal or Bangla Desh; in those Eastern European places, neither the individual nor the nation has hardly anything worth the name of liberty. And it is hard to believe, in their case, that there could ever be freedom for one without freedom for all. The reasons for the presence of Russian tanks in the streets of Czechoslovakia today are said to be different from those which prompted the entry of Persian ships into the waters of ancient Greece: the enlargement of empire is no longer a motive that men will acknowledge: the Russian tanks are in Prague for 'the security and the common good of socialism'; the people are gripped in a vice which claims to be the embrace of fraternal solicitude. For those who endure this new style of alien oppression, there is no ambiguity about their conception of liberty, any more than there was doubt for those early Greeks who contrasted their freedom with the Persian presence. Only people who are in some sense free worry and argue about the meaning of freedom: to those who are enslaved its meaning is luminously clear.

Rousseau's
Social Contract

The *Social Contract* is, as Rousseau explains in his preface, a fragment of something much more ambitious – a comprehensive work on *Institutions politiques* which he began to write in 1743 but never finished. In 1743 Rousseau was thirty-one years old, and working as private secretary to the Comte de Montaigu, French ambassador to the Venetian Republic. This place gave Rousseau his first intimate acquaintance with politics and government. The ambassador was a retired general with no qualifications or aptitude for diplomacy. Rousseau, who was quick and capable, and could speak Italian, performed the duties of Embassy secretary. Unfortunately, he had no official status; he was not a diplomatist; he was the ambassador's personal employee; he was, as the ambassador tactlessly reminded him from time to time, a domestic servant. Rousseau felt cheated and humiliated. To do the work of a diplomatist and be treated like a lackey was unbearable.[1] Within a year, he was gone, dismissed, and not even given his promised wages.

What made the Comte de Montaigu's attitude the more unbearable to Rousseau was not only the injustice, but also the underlying reality: Jean-Jacques *was* a servant, and he had never been anything much better. He had the soul and the mind, as the whole world was soon to recognize, of an exceptional and superior being, but his rank and condition were humble. He had been born in Geneva on 28 June 1712, the second son of Isaac Rousseau, a spirited and irresponsible

1. Indeed Voltaire put about the false story that Rousseau had been the Ambassador's valet, not his secretary. For evidence of Rousseau's duties at the Embassy see R. A. Leigh, ed., *Correspondance complète de Jean-Jacques Rousseau*, Geneva, 1965 (hereinafter abridged as *Corr. complète*), vols i and ii.

watchmaker of that city. His mother died a few days after giving him birth. He was brought up, together with his elder brother, by an aunt and a nursemaid. Isaac Rousseau, who had a passion for books, entertained his sons by reading them novels, histories and the heroic biographies of Plutarch, so that Rousseau could afterwards boast, 'I was a Roman before I was twelve.' In fact, by the time he was ten, the readings from Plutarch had come to an end; his father had fought a duel as a consequence of which he was compelled to quit Geneva, and the sons were boarded out with a Calvinist pastor and his sister. At the age of thirteen Rousseau was apprenticed to an engraver, at whose house he lived.

'My trade,' he recalled many years later, 'did not displease me in itself . . . I should perhaps have succeeded if the brutality of my master and excessive constraint had not disgusted me with the work.'[1]

Rousseau's very first taste of employment was thus to him an experience of bondage. He had grown up in greater freedom than most children. He had been petted, even spoiled by his father and by the several women who did their best to make up to him for the loss of his mother. Besides, as one of his biographers has noted, Rousseau belonged to a family which had come down in the world, and in his early years 'he suffered from a kind of social down-grading which he was to spend his whole life trying to rectify'.[2] His father had failed as a watchmaker partly because he felt that he was too cultured a man for an artisan's trade and partly because he had not enough strength of character to make the best of his situation. Isaac Rousseau lived in a world of fantasy, he wasted the legacy his wife had left him, and he was finally forced into exile because he insisted on settling a dispute by a 'gentleman's' appeal to the sword. In some ways, perhaps, he was like his son.

One Sunday evening in March 1728, when he was not yet six-teen, Rousseau found himself shut out of Geneva after a walk in the country; he had forgotten the time, and the city gates were closed when he reached them. This had happened to him twice before, and

1. Quoted by Jean Guéhenno in *Jean-Jacques Rousseau*, trans. J. and D. Weightman, London, 2 vols, Routledge, 1966, i, p. 15.
2. Ibid., p. 14.

his master had beaten him for staying out all night. This time he decided he would not go back at all.[1] So his life of wandering began.

In the Catholic principality of Savoy, surrounding the city of Geneva, priests were on the look-out for converts among the young people who came from that Calvinist republic. Not only priests; there were proselytizers also among the laity, including a remarkable woman of thirty, the Baroness de Warens, who lived, separated from her husband, at Annecy, and specialized in helping young men. It was to Madame de Warens that Rousseau was sent by the first Catholic friend he made in Savoy. To his surprise, she was agreeably unlike the usual charitable lady of the parish. 'What I saw was a face that was charm itself; beautiful, blue eyes, full of sweetness; a ravishing complexion; the curve of an enchanting bosom.'[2] Madame de Warens was a romantic as well as a pious woman. Her religious sentiments were never perhaps wholly distinct from erotic feelings; one form of ecstasy merged easily into another; but if her converts and her protégés were sometimes also her lovers, her connexion with the priests protected her from scandal. She even received from the King of Sardinia a pension in recognition of her work for the salvation of young Protestant souls.

Madame de Warens did not immediately detain Rousseau at Annecy. She urged him on to Turin, where he was to renounce his Protestant faith and lodge in a Catholic hospice. Then to earn his keep he was obliged to become a footman. He disliked the experience and, remembering Madame de Warens, went back to Annecy the following summer to seek her patronage. This time she took him into her household and mothered him; he called her *maman* and she called him *petit*. She also arranged for him to have music lessons, and so provided the training for what was sometimes to prove his chief means of earning a living, a bearable alternative to domestic service: work as a music copyist and music teacher.

Madame de Warens also gave Rousseau access to a substantial library, and thus enabled him to educate himself from books. From

1. Less perhaps because he feared a beating than because he yearned for adventure. See Georges May, *Rousseau par lui-même*, Paris, 1963, p. 8.

2. *Confessions*. See *Œuvres complètes*, Bibliothèque de la Pléiade, Paris, 1959-65 (hereinafter abridged as 'Pléiade'), i, 49.

time to time, Rousseau wandered away from Madame de Warens's house, working for other employers, travelling in search of adventures, seeking his identity,[1] but he always returned to what was the only home he had. When he was twenty, Madame de Warens decided, as Rousseau puts it, 'to treat me as a man'. The affair lasted for six years; then Rousseau discovered that Madame de Warens had taken another lover, one Winzenried. Gradually, Rousseau's life ceased to centre on her house in the Savoy. While working as a tutor in the family of Monsieur de Mably, brother of the socialist theorist, the Abbé de Mably, Rousseau conceived the idea of becoming a writer, and this ambition prompted him to seek his fortune in Paris.

Rousseau's first problem as a budding writer was to discover the medium in which to express what he had to say. He had never any doubt that a writer's mission was to give verbal expression to the truth; at the same time he felt that the truth was melancholy and disturbing. He had also the familiar problem of a livelihood. When music copying and music lessons did not bring in enough money, he became private secretary to another benefactress, Madame Dupin, wife of a rich taxfarmer. It was through this connexion that Rousseau gained the opportunity to enter what he visualized as the more distinguished world of diplomacy as secretary to the French Ambassador in Venice.

The year in Venice was miserable. The Comte de Montaigu and his secretary got on one another's nerves. Rousseau became increasingly bitter as he felt more exploited, deceived and abused. The Ambassador found Rousseau impudent, churlish and hysterical. They parted, each thinking the other mad and each accusing the other of robbing him. Besides, Rousseau did not much care for Venice or the Venetians. Architecture did not appeal to him, and Venice lacked nature. Its famous courtesans did not provide the kind of love he wanted; one of them advised him to give up women and study mathematics. His chief consolation was the Italian opera, which he adored. As a republican city-state he considered Venice much inferior, politically, to his native Geneva, but at least the

1. This last was perhaps a lifelong quest. See R. Grimsley, *Jean-Jacques Rousseau, a study in self-awareness*, University of Wales Press, 1961.

comparison prompted him to start writing what he himself regarded as his most important book:

Of the different works that I had on the stocks [he wrote long afterwards in his *Confessions*] the one . . . at which I worked with the greatest liking, to which I wished to dedicate myself all my life, and which, in my belief, was to set the seal upon my reputation, was my *Institutions politiques*. . . . I had come to see that everything was radically connected with politics, and that whatever was done about it, no nation would be other than what the nature of its government made it.[1]

After the interlude in Venice, Rousseau made his way back to Paris. He was still angry and indignant about the way he had been treated, but once in Paris his fortunes began to change. He had already made friends with an enterprising contemporary who had come up from the provinces, Denis Diderot, and the two of them talked of taking the literary world of France by storm. Their dreams were extravagant, but in the event their success was far greater than anything they contemplated. Rousseau first made his mark as a musician. He invented a new system of musical notation. It was not accepted by the Academy, but it gained him an award. His *Dissertation sur la musique moderne* was published, and attracted notice. He also composed operas and ballets in the Italian style. His ballet *Les Muses galantes* was performed in Paris in the autumn of 1745, and enjoyed some success in spite of the open scorn of Rameau, the leading French composer of the time. Rousseau's opera *Le Devin du village* was played at Fontainebleau in 1752 before a delighted audience which included the king. Rousseau might then have had a royal pension, but, torn by conflicting emotions, longing for the money but proud and contemptuous of kings, he let slip the opportunity.

Diderot in the meantime was making his name as the editor of what was to prove the most significant literary enterprise of eighteenth-century France, the great *Encyclopédie*. All the leading French intellectuals or *philosophes* contributed to Diderot's pages. Rousseau, too, was a contributor, writing at first on musical and afterwards on other subjects. He found the work difficult. 'I am

1. Pléiade, i, 404.

worn out,' he wrote to Madame de Warens, 'but I have given my promise and one must keep one's word. Besides, I want to get at the throats of people who have treated me badly, and bile gives me strength, even intelligence and knowledge.'[1]

The *Encyclopédie* got Diderot into trouble. He was more of an atheist than Voltaire; he had been trained for the priesthood as a young man, and his anticlerical materialism had the sharp edge of apostasy. Under pressure from the religious authorities, Diderot was imprisoned in July 1749 at Vincennes. One memorable afternoon, Rousseau went to visit him there. According to the story Rousseau tells in his *Confessions*, he had a singular experience on the journey. He opened a copy of the *Mercure de France* and read the announcement of a prize essay competition on the question 'Has the revival of the arts and sciences done more to corrupt or purify morals?' Rousseau tells us that it came to him as a sudden revelation what the answer was. Hardly able to breathe, let alone walk, he sat under a tree and wept. When he reached Vincennes, he told Diderot what had happened. His friend encouraged him to enter for the essay competition, and uphold the opinion that the revival of the arts and sciences had only corrupted morals. Diderot did not agree with this at all, but he was a born journalist, and he suggested that such an unfashionable belief would distinguish Rousseau from the other competitors and capture the prize. Diderot was right. Rousseau submitted his essay and won; henceforth, whether he liked it or not, he was a famous man.

The subject of the Dijon essay was nicely designed to make Rousseau realize how different from other men's his opinions were, different not only from those of the majority, but from those of Diderot and the other *philosophes* of the Enlightenment. Whether it is true that it all came to him suddenly on the road to Vincennes or whether the thoughts had been slowly maturing in his head for years, Rousseau had now worked out a *Weltanschauung* which was distinctively his own, and which put him at odds with all the prevailing streams of eighteenth-century opinion, both religious and materialistic.

1. Rousseau to Madame de Warens, 27 January 1749, *Corr. complète*, ii, 113. Among the throats Rousseau aimed at was that of the composer Rameau.

Diderot and the other *philosophes* were all disciples of the English philosopher Francis Bacon. They believed in progress: more precisely they believed that the development and organization of empirical knowledge could immeasurably improve the life of man on earth. Science would save us. Two steps were needed to realize this project. First, superstition must be banished; traditional philosophy, that unscientific amalgam of Christianity and Aristotle, must be swept away to clear the path to real knowledge. Secondly, the pursuit of such real or empirical knowledge had to be planned, for the conquest of nature was not something that one individual philosopher could accomplish alone in his study; it could only be done by research undertaken by scholars in co-operation. The *Encyclopédie* itself was an example of such collaboration, with experts in different fields each helping to provide a synopsis of all available knowledge. The object was not merely an academic one; as Diderot wrote in the preface to the first volume: 'Our aim is to gather all knowledge together, so that our descendants, being better instructed, may become at the same time happier and more virtuous.'[1]

Rousseau, in his first prize essay, attacked all these Baconian notions. Science was not saving us; it was bringing moral ruin on us. Progress was an illusion. What appeared to be advancement was in reality retrogression. The development of modern civilization had not made men either happier or more virtuous. Happiness belonged to man's life in a state of nature. Virtue was possible in a simple society, where men lived austere and frugal lives. In modern sophisticated society man was corrupted, and the greater the sophistication the greater the corruption.

The arts of civilized societies served only to 'cast garlands of flowers over the chains men bore'. The sciences were the fruit of their vices. Arithmetic, for example, sprang from avarice; physics from idle curiosity; mechanics from ambition. And this evil in the origin of the sciences appeared again in their purposes. If men were not unjust, they would have no use for jurisprudence; if there were no wars or conspiracies or tyrannies, there would be no history. Error was unfortunate, but ignorance did no harm. As for the grand Baconian hope of creating abundance on earth, Rousseau saw more

1. *Encyclopédie*, vol. i, Préface.

evil than good in it. Abundance to him spelt luxury, and luxury was notoriously a breeder of corruption. Frugality, he argued, was equally necessary for a good and upright life in an individual and for a strong and healthy state. Luxury undermined nations as it undermined men.

As an example of a frugal nation Rousseau mentioned Sparta. Throughout his life he continued to regard Sparta as an ideal model of the city-state. Athens he admired less. For Athens had an advanced and sophisticated culture; it made itself a seat of politeness and taste, a city of poets and orators, its buildings as elaborate as its literature. All these Athenian arts and sciences, Rousseau argued, went with moral decay, and he quoted the authority of the Athenian Plato to support him: for had not Plato said that so-called scientific knowledge was not knowledge at all and proposed that poets and artists should be banished from an ideal republic?

To Diderot, a cheerful and tolerant man, these arguments of Rousseau were so many entertaining paradoxes, not to be taken too much to heart. He was inclined to regard them as the product of Rousseau's Swiss origins. Rousseau's love of Sparta and dislike of Athens he saw as an expression of his attachment to Swiss rusticity and estrangement from French civility. And indeed Rousseau's 'rusticity' grew more pronounced when, as a result of winning the Dijon prize, he became a celebrity, and the fashionable hostesses of Paris began to vie with one another for the honour of entertaining him in their *salons*. Diderot, like the other *philosophes*, relished such social success. Rousseau did not. He could get on well with titled ladies on a basis of intimate friendship; Madame de Warens was only the first of a succession of noblewomen who responded to Rousseau's charms and put themselves out to befriend him. But he was painfully ill at ease in the *salons*, in social gatherings that were governed by intricate rules of behaviour. Lacking the appropriate upbringing, Rousseau was paralysed by what he afterwards called a 'false shame'. Refusing to play the part of a literary celebrity in Paris, he began to live what he spoke of as 'a life of solitude'.

He did not, however, live entirely alone. Soon after he returned from Venice to Paris he formed a union with an unusually ignorant laundry-maid named Thérèse le Vasseur, and thereafter she and her mother were part of his permanent household. Thérèse bore him five children, who were all dispatched to an orphanage as soon as they were born. Late in life Rousseau married her. Possibly it was another sign of what Diderot called his 'Swiss rusticity' that the same Rousseau who fled from the *salons* could feel at home in a kitchen with a girl who was backward and stupid and plain. Switzerland had undoubtedly affected his thinking. In one of his polemical writings[1] Rousseau recalled how, as a youth, he had been impressed by a village that stretched up a mountainside near Lake Neuchâtel. There, he said, was a community of little wooden houses, each standing in the centre of the piece of land on which the family depended. Each was about the same size. It was a community of equals. The inhabitants were happy peasants, unburdened by taxes and tithes, who supported themselves by their own work. They were all skilled in a great variety of trades; there was no cabinet-maker, locksmith, glazier or carpenter among them, because every man did all these jobs for himself. They built and maintained their own houses. They also provided their own amusements; they could all dance, sing, and play the flute. Moreover, Rousseau added, their taste – unlike that of modern townsfolk – was good.

Rousseau recalled this mountain community in the course of a controversy with d'Alembert, co-editor with Diderot of the *Encyclopédie*, when d'Alembert had proposed that Geneva should improve its amenities by building a theatre. Rousseau replied protesting, first, that dramatic performances were morally harmful, and secondly, that a healthy culture had no need of theatres. The example he gave of such a sound culture was, significantly, not Geneva itself, but this rural Swiss community which had kept its simplicity, and still lived much as it had lived for hundreds of years; it had been spared the corrupting influence of 'progress'.

Neuchâtel was politically a protectorate of the Prussian crown; in some other Swiss cantons the rustic culture went together with a form of primitive democracy which held for Rousseau a peculiar interest. These cantons were sovereign political societies united in a

---

1. *J-J. Rousseau, Citoyen de Genève, à M. d'Alembert ... sur le Projet d'établir un théâtre de Comédie en cette Ville* in *Collection complète des Œuvres de J-J. Rousseau*, Geneva, 1782, vol. ii.

loose confederation with their neighbours. They were small enough to have the whole adult male population meet at intervals to legislate. This was democracy somewhat on the lines of that of the ancient Greek city-states, and it was something which survived in Europe only in Switzerland. Allemanic democracy was at least as old as Tacitus, who considered it a typically tribal and barbaric institution. It was a form of government which could only exist together with a simple form of culture, a small state, a face-to-face society where everyone knew his neighbours, and where all men were more or less equal.

In other parts of the western world, democracy came to be seen as a progressive, liberal idea; the champions of democracy in America, France and elsewhere were men who wanted to democratize parliamentary or representative government by introducing universal suffrage. The democrats of rural Switzerland had no need to be reformers. They had democracy already, and their only problem was to keep it. The notion of 'representation' was alien to their direct democracy where *every* citizen was a legislator. Indeed, progressive, liberal ideas were seen as a threat to Swiss democracy, for they went together with the movement to centralize Switzerland, to set up a national parliament, and merge the independence of the cantons in a large modern state. Democracy in rural Switzerland went logically together with a conservative, even a reactionary disposition; and it should not astonish us to find in Rousseau a similar belief in legislation by the citizens *en masse* coupled with hostility to progressive and liberal opinions.[1]

In 1754, when he was forty-two, Rousseau wrote a second essay for the Academy of Dijon. This one, which failed to win the prize, was on the question: 'What is the origin of inequality among men, and is it authorized by natural law?' What he wrote had more bearing on the first part of the question than it had on the second.

---

1. 'When we see among the happiest people in the world bands of peasants regulating the affairs of state under an oak tree, and always acting wisely, can we help feeling a certain contempt for the refinements of other nations, which employ so much skill and mystery to make themselves at once illustrious and wretched?' (*The Social Contract*, book iv, ch. 1.) The Swiss cantons are not named, but the reference is obviously to them.

His *Discours sur l'origine de l'inégalité parmi les hommes* is largely historical; the question of right and law he reserved for the *Social Contract*, and by the time he came to write the later work his views had to some extent changed. In the *Discours sur l'inégalité* Rousseau depicts the state of nature as one of innocence. What distinguishes men from beasts is first their faculty of self-improvement and secondly man's only natural moral quality, which is compassion or sympathy. In the state of nature, man lives alone. It is when he becomes sociable that he becomes wicked. In the early stages, when each begins working together with other men in hunting or in joint defence against natural disasters, association sharpens man's feelings of sympathy, and so breeds notions of considerations and obligation. But other things also happen. The cultivation of the earth leads to the enclosure of land, and this necessarily gives rise to the idea of property. As Rousseau puts it in a famous sentence: 'The first man who, after fencing off a piece of land, took it upon himself to say "This belongs to me" and found people simple-minded enough to believe him, was the true founder of civil society.'[1]

Rousseau explains what he means in this way: once men begin to claim possessions, the inequality of men's talents and skills leads to an inequality of fortunes. Wealth enables some men to enslave others; the very idea of possession excites men's passions, and provokes conflict. Society breeds war. This leads in turn to a demand for a system of law to impose order and tranquillity. The rich especially voice this demand, for while the state of violence threatens everyone's life, it is worse for the rich because it threatens their possessions also. Hence the agreement between men to live under a political system.

Such was, or may have been, the origin of civil society and laws, which gave new fetters to the poor, and new powers to the rich; which destroyed natural liberty for ever, fixed for all time the law of property and inequality, transformed shrewd usurpation into settled right, and to benefit a few ambitious persons, subjected the whole of the human race thenceforth to labour, servitude and wretchedness.[2]

1. Pléiade, iii, 164.
2. Ibid., p. 178.

The effect of the establishment of political societies is both to institutionalize and increase inequalities. The establishment of such things as property rights and titles of nobility sets the seal of law on inequality. But 'even without the intervention of government, inequality of credit and authority became unavoidable among private persons as soon as their union in the same society led them to compare themselves one to another'.[1] In the end society reaches a point where men come to be satisfied with themselves rather on the testimony of other people than on their own. Where the savage 'lives within himself', the social man 'lives constantly outside himself, and knows how to live only in the opinion of others; he acquires, so to speak, the consciousness of his own existence only from the judgement of others'.[2] Rousseau suggests, however, that things need not have turned out as badly as they have. If, with the establishment of government, men 'ran headlong into chains', that was because men had the sense to see the advantages of political institutions, but not the experience to foresee the dangers. To this theme Rousseau was to return some years later in the *Social Contract*.

When the *Discours sur l'inégalité* was published in September 1755 it carried a dedicatory epistle to the Republic of Geneva, a fulsome tribute to the author's native city:

Having had the happiness to be born among you, how could I meditate on the equality which nature has set between men and the inequality which they themselves have instituted, without reflecting on the profound wisdom by which equality and inequality, happily combined in that Republic, are balanced in the manner that is most in conformity with natural law, and most favourable to society, to the maintenance of government and to the happiness of individuals.[3]

This gesture was one of Rousseau's manoeuvres to recover his rights as a citizen of Geneva. Already at the age of fifteen he had proudly scribbled his name on a country gate: '*Jean-Jacques Rousseau, citoyen de Genève*, 1727'. As the son of a citizen he would normally have been entitled to become one also, but when he

1. Pléiade, iii, 188–9.
2. Ibid., p. 193.
3. Ibid., p. 111.

adopted the Catholic faith in Savoy, he forfeited the right, and it was only when he formally returned to the Calvinist fold that he was able to regain it. His association with Thérèse made the Protestant pastor hesitate to administer Holy Communion, but Rousseau protested that Thérèse was only his servant, and in his dedicatory epistle to the Republic of Geneva he went out of his way to proclaim his belief in chastity: 'Lovable and virtuous daughters of the city, it will always be the destiny of your sex to govern ours. Happy we are, so long as your chaste power, exercised solely within the marriage tie, is exercised only for the glory of the state and the happiness of the people.'[1] Rousseau had not yet put his own union with Thérèse 'within the marriage tie'; but he could plausibly argue that the disease by which he was increasingly afflicted – a constriction of the bladder which forced him to wear a catheter – disabled him from fornication.

Rousseau's stay in Geneva was brief, and any illusions he may have had of finding a congenial form of government in that city were soon removed. Seven years later, when his *Social Contract* and *Émile* were published, both books were burned by the government of Geneva and a warrant issued for the arrest of the author, notwithstanding the fact that the *Social Contract* contained several flattering references to Geneva, notably in the preface to Book i where Rousseau writes: 'Whenever I reflect on governments, I am happy to find that my studies always give me fresh reasons for loving that of my own country.'

It is not difficult to imagine why the *Social Contract* offended the authorities of Geneva. In theory the city was a republic, and the *Social Contract* is an intensely republican book. But in practice Geneva was a patrician gerontocracy, dominated by a few families. It was an example of what is castigated by Rousseau as the worst form of constitution, that is one in which the sovereignty has passed from the people into the hands of an hereditary aristocracy.

The twelve years between the winning of the Dijon prize for his *Discours sur les sciences et les arts* when he was thirty-eight and the publication of the *Social Contract* when he was fifty formed the

---

1. Ibid., p. 119.

most creative period of Rousseau's life, in spite of the fact that he suffered during this same period from almost constant pain because of the urinary disease. He worked on *Émile* and his novel, *La Nouvelle Héloïse*, at the same time as he was working on the *Social Contract*. In the same twelve years he wrote, besides his *Discours sur l'inégalité* his *Lettre à d'Alembert sur les spectacles*, his attack on the stage, his *Lettre à Voltaire sur la providence*, a defence of religious faith as a rejoinder to Voltaire's *Poème sur le désastre de Lisbonne*; he wrote his *Lettre sur la musique française* to promote the natural melodic style of Italian music against the intellectual, artificial French style (and particularly against the music of Rameau); and he wrote his *Essai sur l'origine des langues*, developing a theory of language and society, which has inspired the structuralists of our own times.

During these productive years, Rousseau had lived in the country some little distance from Paris, first at L'Hermitage, a cottage in the park of Madame d'Épinay, and afterwards at Montmorency, on the estate of another patron, the Maréchal de Luxembourg. He was deeply wounded when Diderot, as he imagined, mocked him for leading this secluded way of life: 'Only the bad man lives alone,' says a character in Diderot's play, *Le Fils naturel*.[1] In any case, Rousseau's rural peace came to an end in 1762, when *Émile* was condemned by the *parlement* of Paris, and the author had to flee from France to avoid arrest. He went to Bernese territory in Switzerland, where he learned that he was a wanted man in Geneva as well as in France. Then he was expelled from the canton of Berne. He had offended almost everyone: Catholics, Protestants, materialists. And so, the last unhappy phase of his life began, when, as the victim of political and religious intolerance, he was harried from place to place in search of refuge.

The political views of the *philosophes* were as distasteful to Rousseau as were most of their opinions. Like their master, Francis Bacon, they believed in strong government; the doctrine of planning called

1. For Diderot's version of the story see A. M. Wilson, *Diderot*, Oxford University Press, 1957, pp. 254ff. The incident led to a final rift between the two writers.

for a ruler with enough power to put plans into effect; and just as Bacon himself once dreamed of converting James I to his way of thinking and then using magnified royal prerogative to enact his proposals, so the *philosophes* of the eighteenth century based their hopes for success on influencing powerful monarchs to do what they suggested. The current name for this was *le despotisme éclaire*; to Rousseau, the champion of freedom, any kind of despotism was anathema, and the so-called enlightened sort was, if anything, worse than others.

In 1755 Rousseau addressed a letter to a pastor in Geneva who had conceived the idea of launching a literary periodical: 'Believe me, Sir, this is not the sort of work for you,' he wrote. 'Serious and profound writings may do us credit, but the glitter of that trivial philosophy which is fashionable today is wholly unbecoming to us. Great themes such as virtue and liberty enlarge and fortify the mind; little things, like poetry and the fine arts, give it more delicacy than subtlety.'[1]

The great themes of liberty and virtue were the themes of the *Social Contract*. This is why Rousseau attached so much importance to the book; and also, perhaps, why it got him into trouble. It might seem to the reader that Rousseau started to write the *Social Contract* as a book about liberty and ended up with a book about virtue; in truth it is the argument of the whole book that once men have entered into society, freedom comes to be inseparable from virtue. Some time between the writing of the *Discours sur l'inégalité* and the writing of the *Social Contract*, Rousseau read – or re-read – the works of Hobbes. His only reference in the *Social Contract* to Hobbes are fleeting and hostile ones, but Professor Robert Derathé[2] has shown that Rousseau was not in the habit of acknowledging his intellectual debts, and that his debts were particularly great both to the legal theorists, or jurisconsults, of earlier generations, to Grotius,[3]

1. Rousseau to Jacob Vernes, 2 April 1755; quoted in G. May, *op, cit.*, p. 26.

2. R. Derathé, *Jean-Jacques Rousseau et la science politique de son temps*, Paris, 1950.

3. Hugo Grotius (1583–1645), Dutch jurist; author of *De jure belli et pacis* (1625).

Pufendorf,[1] Barbeyrac,[2] and Burlamaqui,[3] and also to the political philosophers, especially Hobbes and Locke. The second title of Rousseau's *Social Contract* is the same as the main title of one of Burlamaqui's books: *Principes du droit politique*. This *droit politique*, which one feels obliged for lack of a better alternative (there is no English equivalent of *le droit*) to translate as 'political right', Burlamaqui employed as a semi-technical expression to designate the general abstract study of law and government, and Rousseau generally uses the word in the same sense.[4]

The main title of Rousseau's *Social Contract* refers to a concept which all these jurisconsults and political philosophers invoked. They all believed that the state was the outcome of a covenant or agreement among men. The purpose of the state was the protection of those people to which it owed its being, and the same theorists also agreed that the sovereign must have enough power to provide such protection. Most of the theorists sought at the same time to limit this power of sovereigns under one principle or another, and even to divide sovereignty between several elements. Hobbes stood apart from the others in insisting that sovereignty must be unified and absolute. Hobbes said that men must choose: either they were ruled or they were free; they could not be both; liberty went with anarchy and security with civil obedience. Rousseau accepted Hobbes's argument on one point; he agreed that sovereignty must be absolute or nothing, but he could not bring himself to accept Hobbes's notion that men must choose between being governed and being free. Rousseau, who loved liberty so much, believed he could show that it was possible for men to be at once free and members of

1. Samuel Pufendorf (1632–94), German jurist; author of *Elementa jurisprudentiae universalis* (1660), *De jure naturae et gentium* (1672), *De officio hominis et civis* (1673).

2. Jean Barbeyrac (1674–1744), French jurist, translator and commentator on the works of Grotius and Pufendorf.

3. Jean-Jacques Burlamaqui (1694–1748), Genevan jurist; author of *Principes du droit naturel* (1747), *Principes du droit politique* (1754).

4. Generally but not always. For a discussion of the meaning of the word '*droit*' in Rousseau, see W. Pickles: 'Rousseau and the Problem of Time' in M. Cranston and R. Peters, eds. *Hobbes and Rousseau*, New York, Doubleday, London, Macmillan, 1972.

a political society. Indeed the *Social Contract* may be read as an answer to Hobbes by an author whose mind was stimulated by the brilliance of Hobbes's reasoning, but who could not stomach Hobbes's conclusion.

It is important to note what Rousseau is doing in the *Social Contract*. He explains it clearly at the beginning: 'My purpose is to consider *if*, in political society, there can be any legitimate and sure principle of government, taking men as they are, and laws as they might be.' The *if* is crucial. Rousseau is not offering a plan for reform,[1] nor is he writing the kind of history and sociology he provides in his *Discours sur l'inégalité*. He is dealing with *right* rather than with *fact*, though fact comes into it, because he undertakes to deal with men 'as they are'. In the *Social Contract* Rousseau is writing, in the hypothetical mood, about abstract problems which seem to him to emerge from philosophical reflection on the actual nature of man and the possible order of laws and government. The contract discussed in the *Social Contract* is not the actual historical contract described in the *Discours sur l'inégalité*, that *imposture*[2] made to consolidate the advantages of the rich. It is a genuine and legitimate contract, which is to the benefit of everyone, since it unites liberty with law and utility with right.

Rousseau not only rejects Hobbes's claim that men must choose between being free and being ruled, he positively asserts that it is only through living in civil society that men can experience their fullest freedom. This is the connexion between freedom and virtue. Here we may detect a modification of the argument of the *Discours sur l'inégalité*. In the earlier work Rousseau stresses both the freedom and the innocence of man in the state of nature. In the *Social Contract* he still says that men have freedom in the state of nature, but he treats it as freedom of a crude and lesser kind. Such freedom is no more than independence. And while he does not accept Hobbes's picture of man in the state of nature as an aggressive and

1. Rousseau deals with practical politics in his *Projet de Constitution pour la Corse* (written 1764–5) and his *Considérations sur le gouvernement de Pologne* (written June 1771).

2. For a discussion of this see J. Starobinski, 'Du discours de l'inégalité au Contrat social' in *Journées d'Étude sur le Contrat Social*, Paris, 1964.

rapacious being, Rousseau (remembering Hobbes) speaks less of the innocence and more of the brutishness of man in a state of nature. Man in the state of nature, as he is depicted in the *Social Contract*, is a 'stupid and unimaginative animal'; it is only by coming into a political society that he becomes 'an intelligent being and a man'. Assuredly, as a result of the growth of passions and sophistry which society breeds, men have generally grown worse with the passage of time; but that is because society, instead of improving men, has corrupted them. Society is bound to change men, and if it does not do what it is meant to do, and improve them, it will worsen them. Nevertheless, according to Rousseau, it is only by leaving the state of nature and becoming a social being in the fullest sense, that is to say, in becoming a citizen, that man can realize his own nature as man.

Rousseau never abandons the belief, put forward in his *Discours sur l'inégalité*, that men are happy in the state of nature. He continues to think it possible for them to be good. Men cannot, however, be virtuous in the state of nature, virtue being a characteristic of men who are conscious of morality. Unlike Hobbes, Rousseau does not suggest that it is fear which drives men to quit the state of nature; but he does say that it is man's weakness which makes him social.[1] Rousseau also suggests both that Providence has to intervene by creating natural disasters and shortages to force men to co-operate and also that there is a certain natural pressure within men to actualize those social and moral qualities which are mere potentialities in a state of nature.

Here one might suspect a certain equivocation in Rousseau's use of the word 'nature'. But what he is saying is that the state of nature is man's *original* state, not his natural state; for man can only realize his full nature as a man by making the social compact and living under law. Rousseau's ambiguity reflects a common ambiguity in the word 'nature', which is sometimes used to refer to what is, and sometimes to refer to what should be. Rousseau uses the word 'nature' at different times in either of these two senses.

1. 'It is the weakness of man which renders him social: it is our common miseries which carry our hearts towards humanity.' *Émile*, book iv, p. 249, Paris, 1924.

In a way, Rousseau's solution to the problem posed by Hobbes is wonderfully simple. Men can be both ruled and free if they rule themselves. For what is a free man but a man who rules himself? A people can be free if it retains sovereignty over itself, if it enacts the rules or laws which it is obliged to obey. Obligation in such circumstances is wholly distinct from bondage; it is a moral duty which draws its compulsion from the moral will within each man. In this argument, we can detect a striking departure from the 'social contract' theorists who preceded Rousseau. The jurisconsults and Hobbes and Locke all rejected the well-established theories that sovereignty was based on nature or on divine right, and they all argued in one way or another that sovereignty derived its authority from the assent of the people. But these earlier theorists also held that sovereignty was transferred from the people to the ruler as a result of the social contract. Rousseau is original in holding that no such transfer of sovereignty need or should take place: sovereignty not only originates in the people; it ought to stay there.[1]

Rousseau's solution to the problem of how to be at the same time ruled and free might plausibly be expressed as democracy. We have noticed the importance to him of what is commonly named 'democracy' in Switzerland. But Rousseau himself used the word in a rather distinctive fashion,[2] because of the emphasis he puts on the difference between the two departments, as he sees them, of government. Ruling, in the strict sense of making rules or laws, is the function which he says that the people must retain; for thus, and only thus, does sovereignty express itself. Every act of the sovereign is a law, and anything which is not a law is not an act of sovereignty. From this function of law-making, Rousseau distinguishes the administration, or executive management, of government. And he does *not* demand, as a prerequisite of liberty and legitimacy, that this administration shall be conducted by the whole body of citizens. On

---

1. See Derathé, *op. cit.*, p. 47.
2. In a letter to Madame d'Épinay, dated March 1756, Rousseau wrote: 'Learn my dictionary, my good friend, if you want to have us understand each other. Believe me, my terms rarely have the ordinary sense.' Quoted in C. W. Hendel, *Citizen of Geneva: Selected letters of Jean-Jacques Rousseau*, New York, Oxford University Press, 1937, p. 140.

the contrary, he thinks it might be best done by a limited number. The conduct of administration by the whole body of the citizens he seems to consider too utopian an arrangement. This is the arrangement which in the *Social Contract* he calls 'democracy', and of which he is thinking when he says that democracy is for gods, not men.[1]

Rousseau is undoubtedly a democrat in the sense that 'democracy' means legislative rule by the whole body of the citizens; but as he himself used the word in another sense, it might be less confusing to speak of him as a 'republican' or champion of 'popular sovereignty'. One of the reasons why he distinguishes so carefully between the legislative sovereign body and the executive or administrative body is his consciousness of the abiding danger to the legislative which the administrative body constitutes. For while it is convenient that the business of government should be entrusted to a council of magistrates or commissioners, those magistrates will naturally tend, with the passage of time, to encroach on the sacred territory of legislation, and thus to invade the sovereignty and destroy the republican nature of the state. As a matter of empirical fact, Rousseau even suggests that this is bound to happen.[2]

Nowhere in the *Social Contract* does Rousseau offer any short

1. See Book iii, ch. 4.
2. Bertrand de Jouvenel has drawn attention to a contradiction here between Rousseau as a philosopher and Rousseau as a political scientist. Rousseau the political philosopher argues that legitimate government is possible only if sovereignty remains in the hands of the citizens. Rousseau the political scientist puts forward as an empirical law of development that the executive or administrative body must in the long run invade the legislative body and capture the sovereignty. Jouvenel cites a passage from Rousseau's *Lettres écrites de la montagne* (Part 1, Letter 6): '... since sovereignty tends always to slacken, the government tends always to increase its power. Thus the executive body must always in the long run prevail over the legislative body; and when the law is finally subordinate to men, there remains nothing but slaves and masters, and the republic is destroyed.' Jouvenel stresses that the 'must' in this paragraph is a scientific must; so that Rousseau the political scientist is denying the possibility of the continued existence in the real world of the one form of political association which unites liberty with government. See B. de Jouvenel on 'Rousseau' in *Western Political Philosophers*, ed. M. Cranston, London, Bodley Head, New York, Putnam, 1964, and Jouvenel's introduction to his edition of *Du Contrat social*, Geneva, 1947.

definition of liberty, although there are several often-quoted epigrams about it. In his *Lettres écrites de la montagne* (published two years after the *Social Contract*) he provides the most succinct account of what he means by this key word:

> Liberty consists less in doing one's own will than in not being subject to that of another; it consists further in not subjecting the will of others to our own. . . . In the common liberty no one has a right to do what the liberty of any other forbids him to do; and true liberty is never destructive of itself. Thus liberty without justice is a veritable contradiction. . . . There is no liberty, then, without laws, or where any man is above the laws. . . . A free people obeys, but it does not serve; it has magistrates, but not masters; it obeys nothing but the laws, and thanks to the force of the laws, it does not obey men.[1]

It is partly because of this intimate connexion between liberty and law that the freedom of man in a state of nature is so inferior. The freedom of the savage is no more than independence; although Rousseau speaks of the savage being subject to natural law, he also suggests that the savage has no consciousness of natural law; thus Rousseau can speak of a man being 'transformed', as a result of his entry into civil society, from a brutish into a human, moral being. A moral being is, or can be, free in another sense than the political; if, instead of being a slave of his passions, he lives according to conscience, lives according to rules he imposes on himself, then he has a liberty which only a moral being can enjoy. The savage has no sense of this; for one thing, the passions only begin to develop with society, which explains why society can mark the beginning of a change for the worse as well as the beginning of a change for the better. One of the new passions which emerges with society is pride or *amour-propre*, which Rousseau sees as an evil mutation of the perfectly innocent sentiment of self-love or *amour-de-soi*. It is a characteristic of modern sophisticated culture to be dominated by pride. The emphasis on 'going back to nature' in Rousseau's treatise on education, *Émile*, is the result of his belief that cultural environment, not natural inclination, breeds such harmful passions. Here we may notice a contrast between Rousseau's views and Hobbes's. Whereas Hobbes holds that pride is natural to man, Rousseau holds

1. *Lettres écrites de la montagne*, Letter 8, Pléiade, iii, 841–2.

that it is artificial; whereas Hobbes says that war prevails among men in the state of nature because of men's pride, Rousseau says that war is a product of conflicts about property, and therefore cannot exist in the state of nature, where there is no property.

On the other hand, Rousseau seems to be entirely at one with Hobbes when he says that under the pact by which men enter into civil society everyone makes a total alienation of all his rights. However, it must be remembered that Rousseau regarded this alienation as a form of exchange, and an advantageous one; men give up their natural rights in exchange for civil rights; the total alienation is followed by a total restitution; and the bargain is a good one because what men surrender are rights of dubious value, unlimited by anything but an individual's own powers, rights which are precarious and without a moral basis; in return men acquire rights that are limited but legitimate and invincible. The rights they alienate are rights based on might; the rights they acquire are rights based on law.

It might be supposed that Rousseau is contradicting Locke when he says that men alienate all their rights when they make the social contract, Locke having said that men make the social contract only to preserve their rights. But Rousseau is really thinking in different terms from Locke. Rousseau does not think that men have in the state of nature the kind of natural rights which Locke supposes – the right, for example, to property. For Rousseau there is only *possession* in the state of nature; property (by definition, rightful possession) comes into being only when law comes into being. Nor does Rousseau think, like Locke, of liberty as one of men's rights. Indeed he says, quite as emphatically as Locke, that men *cannot* alienate their liberty. If Locke and Rousseau were thinking in the same terms, it would be a contradiction for Rousseau to say, as he does, that the social contract entails the total alienation of rights, and that men cannot alienate their liberty. In truth, what Rousseau is saying is that instead of surrendering their liberty by the social contract, they *convert* their liberty from independence into political and moral freedom, and this is part of their transformation from creatures living brutishly according to impulse into men living humanly according to reason and conscience.

There is no more haunting paragraph in the whole of the *Social*

Contract than that in which Rousseau speaks of forcing a man to be free.[1] But it would be wrong to put too much weight on these words, in the manner of those who consider Rousseau, whether early-fascist or early-communist, at all events a totalitarian.[2] Rousseau is nothing so simple. He is authoritarian, but the authority he favours is explicitly distinguished from mere power; it is based on conscious and vocal assent, and is offered as something wholly consistent with liberty. There is no necessary antithesis, as some writers assume, between liberty and authority as such; for authority is a form of potency which is by definition legitimate and which rests on the credence and acceptance of those who respect it, and Rousseau insists that if authority is to be authentic the credence and acceptance must be both universal and unconstrained. There is no resemblance between Rousseau's republic and the actual systems of twentieth-century totalitarian states, where the various devices of party rule, government by edict, brain-washing and secret police are manifestations of what Rousseau regarded as despotism and vigorously condemned. Indeed for those who seek the theoretical ancestry of present day totalitarian ideology, the optimistic *despotisme éclairé* of the *philosophes* may well be worth as much attention as the pessimistic republicanism of Rousseau.

Rousseau does not say that *men* can be forced to be free in the sense that a whole community may be forced to be free; he says that *a* man may be forced to be free, and he is thinking here of the occasional individual who, as a result of being enslaved by his passions, disobeys the voice of the law, or of the general will, within him. The general will is something inside each man as well as in society as a whole, so that the man who is coerced by the community for a breach of the law, is, in Rousseau's view of things, being brought back to an awareness of his own true will. Thus in penalizing a law-breaker, society is literally correcting him, 'teaching him a lesson' for which, when he comes to his senses, the offender

1. Book i, ch. 7.
2. See, for example, J. L. Talmon, *The Origins of Totalitarian Democracy*, London, Secker and Warburg, 1952. For a rejoinder to Talmon see R. A. Leigh, 'Liberté et autorité dans le Contrat social' in *Jean-Jacques Rousseau et son œuvre*, Paris, 1963.

will be grateful. Legal penalties are a device for helping the individual in his own struggle against his own passions, as well as a device for protecting society against the antisocial depredations of lawbreakers. This explains the footnote to Chapter 2 of Book iv of the *Social Contract*, where Rousseau writes: 'In Genoa the word *Libertas* may be seen on the doors of all the prisons and on the fetters of the galleys. This use of the motto is excellent and just.'

In arguing thus, Rousseau may be seen as adopting and elaborating an argument used by Locke against Hobbes. Hobbes in his plain, robust way, says that to be free is to be unopposed and unconstrained in doing what one wants to do; the law is a form of constraint, so that the less the law forbids, the more free a man is: 'The liberty of the subject is the silence of the laws.' Locke rejects this; he holds that the law does not diminish men's freedom, but effectively enlarges it, both by protecting a man from anarchic invasions of his liberty and by preventing collisions between one man's use of his liberty and another's. Locke even accepts the notion, though he never uses the words, of forcing a man to be free, because he mentions the case of a man who is prevented by *force majeure* from crossing a bridge which is dangerous and which he does not know to be dangerous; as soon as the man learns the true situation, he is grateful to those who have taken hold of him, and no longer feels that his freedom has been invaded. This is the kind of situation that Rousseau has in mind – albeit on a much larger scale – when he speaks of forcing a man to be free. The recalcitrant, to Rousseau, is someone who is out of joint with himself and with society, and thus to use physical restraint on him is not to harm, or injure, him, but, on the contrary, to help or heal, to recover him for reason, and therefore, at the same time, for freedom. It is difficult, assuredly, to reconcile this way of thinking with Rousseau's partiality for the death penalty.

In the discussion of liberty, Rousseau's whole emphasis is different from Locke's. Locke is not worried, as Rousseau is, by corruption; and he does not hanker after any republican ideal of virtue. Locke thinks that a system of positive law set up by a constitutional state can enlarge men's liberty, but he also thinks that many systems of positive law do diminish men's liberty. For Locke there are good laws and bad laws. Good laws are the ones that recognize and defend men's natural rights, bad laws are the ones that neglect or abuse those rights. And therefore for Locke the problem is to have positive laws that secure men's rights and avoid laws that imperil men's liberty. But Rousseau has a different approach, or rather he has two distinctive approaches to law. When he is speaking of law as right, a law, for him, is by definition just; and even when he characterizes a law as an expression of the general will, it is still by definition just because the general will is by definition rightful. But, secondly, when Rousseau is thinking about the kinds of law he sees in the real world, when he is thinking, so to speak, as an empirical social scientist, he notes that all actual systems of law can be seen to be unjust. In a footnote to Book iv of *Émile* he writes: 'The universal spirit of laws in all countries is to favour the stronger against the weaker, and those who have against those who have nothing: this disadvantage is inevitable and without exception.'[1]

There is thus for Rousseau a radical dichotomy between true law and actual law, between law as it should be and law as it is seen in the existing world. And it should not be forgotten that the law he is writing about in the *Social Contract* is law in the true sense. Thus laws, as he explains them in this book, are rules made by a people in its capacity of sovereign and obeyed by the same people in its capacity as subject. Rousseau thinks it axiomatic that such rules will never be oppressive for the simple reason that a people, being at the same time sovereign and subject, would never forge fetters for itself. The only thing he fears is that the people, being ignorant, might forge fetters unwittingly: hence the need for the lawgiver.

The distinction between true law and actual law corresponds to the distinction Rousseau draws between the general will and the will of all. The general will is a normative concept, its connexion with right is a matter of definition. The will of all is an empirical concept; the only test of the will of all is what, in fact, all will. Having been so severe on Grotius for failing to distinguish between fact and right, Rousseau is careful not to make the same mistake himself.

Why should I abide by the decision of the majority? Because by the social contract itself, to which *everyone* subscribes and pledges

1. *Émile*, Paris, Classiques Garnier, 1924, p. 270.

(there is no question of a majority here; you either subscribe or you are not in civil society at all), everyone agrees to accept the decision of the majority in the formulation of the law. But it is also understood that the members of the majority whose decision is accepted do not ask themselves what do *I*, as an individual, demand, but what does the general will demand; thus it is the majority *interpretation* of the general will which is binding and not the majority will. This is how it can be morally obligatory for the minority to accept.

Rousseau borrows from Hobbes the argument that sovereignty is an absolute power; it cannot be divided and remain sovereign; and it cannot be subject to 'fundamental laws' and remain sovereign. At the same time Rousseau takes from Locke and the jurisconsults the notion that sovereignty is limited. Sovereignty is absolute, but not unlimited. The limits are those imposed by natural law and by the considerations of public good. 'Sovereignty does not pass the bounds of public advantage.' As an example of what Rousseau means by a natural law limitation, we may note his argument in the *Social Contract* that no agreement to enter into slavery could be a valid one because any agreement which is wholly to the advantage of one party and wholly to the disadvantage of the other is void in natural law.

Several commentators, including C. E. Vaughan,[1] say that Rousseau eliminates natural law, but Professor Derathé has drawn attention to certain passages from Rousseau's writing which illustrate the importance he attaches to natural law. Derathé quotes Rousseau's claim, in the course of his controversy with d'Alembert, that he recognizes three authorities higher than the sovereign authority of the state: 'that of God, that of the natural law which derives from the constitution of man, and that of honour'.[2] Again, in the *Lettres écrites de la montagne* Rousseau writes: 'It is no more permissible to violate natural law by the social contract than it is permissible to violate positive law by private contracts.'[3] Thirdly, in his *Considérations sur le gouvernement de Pologne* (written in 1771), Rousseau

---

1. C. E. Vaughan, *The Political Writings of Jean-Jacques Rousseau*, Cambridge University Press, 2 volumes, 1915.

2. Derathé, *op. cit.*, p. 157.

3. *Lettres écrites de la montagne*, Letter 6, Pléiade, iii, 807.

speaks of '... Natural law, that holy imprescriptable law which speaks to the heart and reason of man. . . .'[1]

Against all this, it must be noticed that Rousseau in the *Social Contract* offers no possibility of an appeal to natural law. It is all very well to say, as he does, that the sovereign must not violate natural law, but this raises the question of who is to be judge of any such violation. In several of his writings, Rousseau emphasizes the supremacy of the individual conscience; he even goes so far as to speak of conscience as infallible. 'Conscience never deceives us.'[2] This might lead one to expect that he would agree with those theorists who hold that the individual conscience must ultimately decide where to draw the line between justice and injustice. In fact, in the *Social Contract* Rousseau takes up the position of Hobbes, namely, that the citizen can have no other guide but the civil law and the public conscience. The general will is itself the arbiter of just and unjust. Here there seems to be a contradiction between the argument of the *Social Contract* and that of the *Profession de foi* and other writings. In the *Social Contract* the general will is the moral authority; elsewhere individual conscience is represented as the innate principle of justice.

This points to another and even more striking contradiction between what Rousseau says in the *Social Contract* and what he says elsewhere. Rousseau as he appears in the *Profession de foi* and indeed in most of his writings, published and unpublished, is clearly a Unitarian or Socinian, like Locke or Malebranche, regarding the minimal creed as a genuine, if not the only genuine, form of Christianity. Rousseau plainly detested the atheism of Diderot and the *philosophes*; his belief in the love of God and the life to come was profoundly important to him. He often said that he could not live without such religious faith. He also believed, much as Locke did, that such Christianity is reasonable.

In the *Social Contract*, however, his attitude is very much closer to that of Machiavelli than it is to that of Locke. What the state needs, Rousseau says in his chapter on the civil religion, is a religion subordinate to the state and designed to teach patriotic,

1. *Political Writings*, ed. C. E. Vaughan, ii, 445.
2. *Profession de foi du vicaire savoyard*, ed. Beauvalon, Paris, 1937, pp. 134–5.

civic and martial virtues. And Christianity, he says, quite as boldly as Machiavelli, is no good for this purpose; it teaches men to love the kingdom of heaven instead of their own republic on earth, and it teaches them to suffer but not to fight. It teaches the wrong virtues. Assuredly, Rousseau makes clear that he is talking here about civil religion, not private religion, and he admits that 'the religion of the Gospel' is the word of God for the private person. But the state religion is the more important, and the state religion must be supreme; Rousseau even goes so far as to propose a death penalty for those whose conduct is at variance with the religious principles they proclaim.

Up to a point Rousseau's argument is perfectly logical; he thinks that men will not become virtuous without the aid of religious institutions – a cult, a church – and since Christianity does not teach the civic virtue that is needed for the kind of republic he favours – a state on the model of Sparta or Rome – Rousseau is entirely consistent in proposing, with Machiavelli, some kind of neo-pagan cult to match the needs of such a state. But how can he reconcile this with his professed faith in Christianity? Conceivably he is saying only that neo-paganism is useful and Gospel Christianity is true, and that the two belong to different logical categories, to be judged by different standards, the one by the standard of social utility and the other by that of truth; but if this is so, Rousseau is putting the useful above the true, and what then becomes of his criticism of his atheistic contemporaries, that they put utility in the place of morality?

An even more serious criticism of Rousseau can, I think, be levelled against his whole theory of liberty. On the one hand, he belongs to a certain tradition of moral philosophers who argue that to be free is not to be left to do what you want to do but to be enabled to do what you ought to do. Everything that Rousseau says about freedom being inseparable from justice, and about the necessary connexion between liberty and virtue, puts him in this school of morality. This theory of freedom, which has its origins in religious thought, claims to offer a superior, higher, more true and exalted analysis of what freedom is. Rousseau stands squarely in this tradition when he speaks of the higher, and more specifically moral freedom that men attain when they quit the state of nature and enter civil society.

But at the same time, Rousseau reveals an attachment to a less exalted idea of what freedom is. This is when he says that freedom is not being subject to any other *man*. Here one may suspect that Rousseau retained from the experiences of his life the simple notion – which might well be the occupational notion of domestic servants – that being dependent on another man is slavery and that freedom is simply having no master. To be dependent on things or institutions is quite different, and wholly unobjectionable. Throughout the *Social Contract* it is clear that Rousseau never sees institutions as a threat to freedom. The image of a king or prince in Rousseau's eyes is the image of a master, and he sees such monarchs as enemies of liberty. But the image of the state touches him quite differently. There is a sentence in Book ii (ch. 12) of the *Social Contract* which illustrates this forcefully: this is where he says that things should be so arranged that every citizen is perfectly independent from all his fellow citizens and 'excessively dependent on the republic'. The word 'excessive' is significant. And why does Rousseau use it? Because he thinks such dependence can never be too great; because dependence on the state guarantees men against all dependence on men, against '*toute dépendance personnelle*'.

Is this a philosopher's concept of freedom? Perhaps; but is it not also like that of a footman? The dream of liberty in the servants' hall is the dream of the elimination of the master; translated into political terms, this becomes the republican fantasy that freedom lies in the elimination of the king. Of course Rousseau says a great deal more than this about freedom. He says that to be free means to live under a law of one's own enactment. But one does not have to progress very far through the pages of the *Social Contract* to see how modest this role of enactment is allowed to become. Men, he insists, are ignorant. The general will is morally sound, it is always rightful, but it is unenlightened. Men cannot be trusted to frame or devise their own laws. They need a Lawgiver to make laws for them. Their part in the enactment of laws is limited to *assent* to those laws. Thus freedom for Rousseau consists of putting oneself willingly under rules devised by someone else.

The measure of confidence that Rousseau has in his fellow men is made clear in *Émile*. At the very end of that long book, when the hero is grown up, and his exemplary education has produced its paragon, the young man, who is married and about to have a child, begs his tutor to stay with him: 'Advise and control us,' he implores the tutor, '. . . as long as I live I shall need you. I need you more than ever now that I am taking on the duties of manhood.'[1]

And just as the Tutor is the dominant figure of *Émile* so does the Lawgiver become the dominant figure of the *Social Contract*. Indeed the Lawgiver repeats in the state the role that the Tutor performs for the individual.[2] He is needed for the same reason; men left alone will be led by their own passions and folly into disaster; they need someone to save them from themselves.

It is a bad thing to have a master; for that is the reverse of freedom. But it is a good thing to have a tutor, so long as we follow him willingly and gladly. For Rousseau the way to liberty is the path of voluntary submission. 'The King is dead; long live the Lawgiver!' Is this, in the end, the battle cry of the republic? Does Rousseau wish us to say: 'Advise and control us, O *Législateur*. As long as we live we shall need you. We need you more than ever now that we are taking on the duties of self-government'?

Many readers may find the *Social Contract* a frustrating book. What is offered with one hand is taken away with the other. It is theoretically possible for a political system to be so devised that men become more free by entering into it. This is to 'take laws as they might be'. On the other hand, it is hard, indeed impossible, to see how such a system could avoid being spoiled. This is to 'take men as they are'. Rousseau enlarges our vision and perhaps also our understanding; at the same time he diminishes our expectations.

1. *Émile*, ed. cit., p. 596.
2. See Judith N. Shklar, 'Rousseau's images of authority', *American Political Science Review*, December 1964, p. 919, and Pierre Burgelin, 'Le social et le politique chez Rousseau' in *Journées d'Étude*, Paris, 1964, p. 173.

Sartre and Violence

In literature, as in other things, there is more than one France. Sartre belongs to the France of Calvin and Pascal and Rousseau, which has always been at odds with the France of Montaigne and Voltaire and Albert Camus. His is the tradition of moral severity and metaphysical intensity, and of puritanical zeal which is often thought to be more Teutonic than French. And it is a fact that Sartre is half-Alsatian; he is a cousin, indeed, of the great Alsatian missionary, Albert Schweitzer. His culture is almost as much German as French, and although his literary ancestory is that of the great French *moralistes*, his system of thought, his existentialism is derived from German models. He was brought up in the house of his grandfather, Karl (or Charles) Schweitzer, an Alsatian Protestant and a scholar, his father having died when Sartre was two years old.

Sartre has sometimes described his own condition as that of a 'false bastard'. He has made some of the heroes of his books real bastards, Edmund Kean in the play *Kean*, for example, and Goetz in *Le Diable et le Bon Dieu*, and he puts forward an elaborate theory of illegitimacy in his book on Jean Genet, which he calls characteristically *Saint Genet*. But one thing is quite clear from Sartre's autobiography. He did not lack a 'father figure' in his childhood. His grandfather enacted the paternal role: he might even be thought to have overacted it. For Karl Schweitzer, with his massive presence and gleaming eye and flowing white beard looked like nothing so much as popular nineteenth-century images of God.

In his home Karl Schweitzer was a stern ruler. Sartre's widowed mother was treated, he tells us, 'like an unmarried daughter who has produced an infant'. Nobody respected her. Only Sartre himself enjoyed the situation; his mother belonged to him, he had no father or brother or sister to 'dispute his peaceful possession of her'. He was spared what he calls 'that harsh apprenticeship – jealousy'.[1] He had, he says, no early experience of hatred and violence. One may well wonder, in view of this, why hatred and violence came to play so large a part in Sartre's writings – not only in the novels and plays, but also his theoretical books and in his politics. Conceivably Sartre was so unfamiliar with violence and hatred in his childhood that when he did meet these things they had a shattering impact.

He recalls that he was a lonely child. But once he had learned to read, books filled his life, and provided a way of living in the imagination for a child who had few companions. It was from books that he learned about the world. But, as he reminds us, the world one learns about from books is an ordered world, assimilated, classified, ticketed, systematic. Learning about the world in this way was responsible, Sartre thinks, for the 'idealism' it took him thirty years to get rid of. He also confesses in his autobiography that he did not relish being alive. He regarded his own birth as a necessary evil. Death became what he calls his *vertige*; it possessed the power of both fascination and dread precisely because he did not like life. In his early fantasies of heroism, death was wedded to glory. He both desired death and feared it. Sartre suggests that this ambivalence lies at the root of most of our deepest intentions: projects and evasions inseparably linked. His own 'mad enterprise' of writing was a way of earning a pardon for living. Writing was his salvation in the sense that it served as a form of expiation for the guilt of being alive.

Much that Sartre has to say about himself in his autobiography is not only expressed in language drawn from religion, but seems somehow to belong to the story of a search for grace. All he tells us about his alienation from his fellow creatures, from life, and from the visible world seems like the first part of the biography of one who finds fulfilment in the contemplation of the invisible world and in the love of God. Indeed, Sartre admits that he might have found God. His grandfather, the son of a Calvinist pastor, was an anticlerical who had only an intermittent faith; his grandmother had a

1. *Les Mots*, Paris, Gallimard, 1964, p. 17.

peacefully worldly disposition. But Sartre's mother was a believer who found a secret consolation in religion, and she sent Sartre to a Catholic priest for instruction. Young Sartre said his prayers. He once even had the sensation of the presence of God. Then his faith petered out. His, he says, was a 'lost vocation'.

When Sartre was aged eleven, his mother married again, and Sartre was then removed to La Rochelle, where his stepfather was in charge of the docks. Sartre thus acquired an early knowledge of French provincial life, and evidently an early hatred of it also. After two years at the local lycée, he was sent to Paris to the Lycée Henri IV. Then, like so many of the leading French intellectuals, he received his academic training at the Ecole Normale Supérieure. Afterwards he became for several years a *professeur de lycée* in the provinces, but spent some time in Berlin studying the work of Husserl, Heidegger, Jaspers, and other contemporary German philosophers. While still a student, Sartre formed his celebrated union with Simone de Beauvoir, a union which, though carefully distinguished from 'bourgeois marriage', nevertheless became a settled partnership in life. His anti-bourgeois opinions in his youth were moral rather than political, and in the election of 1935, when the Popular Front Government was returned, Sartre did not even vote. He believed in the coming victory of socialism, but was content to leave the struggle to others. What interested him then was literature and philosophy, and particularly literature as a medium for the expression of philosophical ideas.

Sartre's first essays in existentialist fiction were his novel *La Nausée* and several short stories collected together as *Le Mur*. *La Nausée* is in no sense political, but intensely philosophical; everything in it turns upon, embodies, or illustrates Sartre's theoretical ideas. It is cast in the form of the diary of one Antoine Roquentin, who is living in the Norman part of Bouville, working on the biography of an eighteenth-century worthy, the Marquis de Rollebon, whose papers are conserved in that place. Roquentin, we might fancy, is a remarkably free man. He is thirty and has a modest private income; no family, no job, none of the so-called 'ties'. He has travelled widely, and can live where he pleases. 'Free' we may want to call him, but it is a part of the argument of the book that

Roquentin is not really free. He is merely non-attached or uncommitted; and it is one of Sartre's central beliefs that non-attachment is only a mockery of freedom, is, indeed, a form of running away from freedom.

Manifestly, Roquentin is not happy (the original title of the novel was *Melancholia*). He has no friends; nobody writes to him; his only conversation is with casual acquaintances. His days are passed in a kind of dull depression, with intermittent spasms of nausea, vertigo, anxiety and other forms of nervous tension which in the Sartrian universe, are not so much symptoms of psychological disorder as intimations of metaphysical reality. The world becomes increasingly unbearable to Roquentin; he feels objects touching him 'as if they were alive', 'as if they were living creatures'. Material objects appear to him as gluey, sticky, viscous. They are all unnecessary, superfluous, 'in the way': they 'inconvenience' him. Human beings equally are superfluous: the same is true of himself: 'And I – soft, weak, obscene, digesting, juggling with dismal thoughts – I, too, was in the way.' Roquentin's uneasiness is metaphysical in the sense that he yearns for the universe to be a harmonious machine as it is in the cosmology of Newton or Leibniz. Where everything was rational, ordered, predictable, where everything was necessary, and had a purpose, where there was a God presiding over all things and a Moral Law demonstrable to all men, where the laws of science were immutable – there, and there alone, would Roquentin feel at ease. This metaphysical malaise is as much the author's as his hero's.

Roquentin begins by assuming that the universe must really be as he wishes it to be: a rational whole, in which the existence of everything is somehow necessary. In the heightened awareness of his 'nausea', he realizes that this is not so. Existence, he discovers, is not an abstract category: it is the 'very paste of things'. The sticky, unformed, half-solid, half-liquid mess which is the physical world as he sees it – this 'paste' alone is reality: there is no higher order of being. One day Roquentin is in a public park gazing at the black root of a chestnut tree. Its blackness, as he perceives it, is not just a colour, it is also 'like a bruise or a secretion, like an oozing – and something else, an odour, for example, of wet earth' or 'a flavour of chewed, sweet fibre'. As he gazes thus at the root, Roquentin feels himself 'plunged into a horrible ecstacy' and it is just then that he understands what his nausea signifies, and hence what existence is. It strikes him 'that the crucial point is *contingency*. I mean that one cannot define existence as necessary. To exist is simply *to be there*.'

Some people may well feel at this point that Sartre protests too much. Roquentin's dramatic discovery that the world is contingent is one that could have been made by any reader of David Hume in the eighteenth century or after. It amounts to little more than the realization that Newton was mistaken. The laws of science – or of Nature – are not fixed laws. The future is not certain to be like the past. In Nature we observe regularities but there is no necessary link between causes and effects. The laws of science are not analytically true, like the laws of mathematics and logic. They are based on statistical uniformities. Because they are contingent they are sometimes inaccurate, and have to be revised.

In all this one may fail to see any reason for excitement, let alone for 'horrible ecstasy'. But if one feels this, one may not appreciate the predicament of Roquentin – or of Sartre. Roquentin is a man to whom questions of metaphysics are questions of life and death. In a universe whose laws are contingent he has no security. He says to himself, 'If this is so, my tongue may turn into a centipede.' In thinking thus, he is plainly giving way to an anxious imagination. Theoretically, everything may be 'possible' in a universe which is not governed by necessary laws; but in a universe which moves in an intelligible and regular way, where natural laws are, though only probable, at any rate reliable, it is a fantastic, even a pathologically morbid thought, that 'my tongue may turn into a centipede'.

And yet to raise this objection is perhaps to speak too readily in the language of common sense, or empiricism, or the Enlightenment. The mentality of existentialism belongs to another order, to romanticism, and indeed historically, to religion. The first existentialist, Kierkegaard, was a passionate Christian, and it was the purpose of his existentialism to suggest that the proof of Christian teaching could never be found in rational arguments but only in the lonely anguish of the sinner separated from God. There are many Christians for whom the thought of living in a universe without a heavenly father is an unthinkable, a terrifying thought. The conditions of Roquentin is akin to theirs. Sartre is an atheist who understands nothing better than man's thirst for God; and whose lesson is that men must learn to live with that thirst for ever unsatisfied.

In *L'Existentialisme est un humanisme* Sartre wrote:

The existentialist is strongly opposed to a certain type of secular moralism which seeks to suppress God at the least possible expense. Towards 1880, when the French professors endeavoured to formulate a secular morality, they said something like this – 'God is a useless and costly hypothesis, so we will do without it . . . nothing will be changed if God does not exist; we shall re-discover the same norms of honesty, progress and humanity, and we shall have disposed of God as an out-of-date hypothesis which will die away quietly of itself.' The existentialist, on the other hand, finds it extremely embarrassing that God does not exist; for there disappears with Him all possibility of finding values in an intelligible heaven. There can no longer be any good *a priori*, since there is no infinite and perfect consciousness to think it.[1]

This profound sense of the absence of God lies at the heart of Sartre's existentialism. It is the explanation of Roquentin's 'abandonment', his 'solitude' and his 'dread'. However, once Roquentin has learned to brace himself to bear this anguish, to face the truth that he lives in a Godless and unNewtonian universe, he discovers one great consolation. If the universe is contingent, it is also free. The future is open. No one is the slave of the past. 'All is free,' he tells himself, 'this park, this city, and myself.'

Sartre is an avowed believer in what he calls 'conversion'. Roquentin's 'conversion' comes when he sees how he might give himself a 'reason for living'. It follows from the contingency of the universe – or the 'absurdity' of the universe as Sartre sometimes expresses it – that no 'reason for living' is given one by God or Nature. Every man must make his own 'reason for living'. Roquentin finds his in art. One day he is listening to an American jazz record, and he imagines a Jewish musician in a hot New York apartment finding a reason for living by creating this simple little tune. Roquentin asks, 'if him, why not I?' His own talent is for writing.

1. *Existentialism and Humanism*, trans. P. Mairet, London, Methuen, 1948, p. 33.

But he tells himself it is no good going on writing biographies: because that is simply to lose one's own being in another's, and 'one existent can never justify the existence of another'. No, it will have to be creative literature: and Roquentin decides to write a novel. It would not be easy, he reflects: 'But a time would come when it would be written, when it would be behind me and I think that a little of its clarity might fall over my own past. Then perhaps because of it, I could remember my life without repugnance.'[1]

La Nausée thus ends on a distinct note of hope: and the source of that hope is the notion of salvation through art. And one can easily see why this idea should appeal to Sartre. In art one creates a world which has what the real world has not. Order, harmony, predictability, the organizing genius of a rational creator – all the characteristics which are lacking – for Sartre painfully lacking – in the real universe, are present in the work of art. Art promises salvation because it offers an escape from the sensible world of contingency into a created world of necessity. Even so, Sartre did not long remain content with this idea of salvation through art.

La Nausée was published in 1938, and was one of the most successful novels of the year. Sartre's short stories attracted no less attention. But the material rewards of success meant little to him, for he had always been an ascetic. Simone de Beauvoir in her memoirs mentions an occasion when she saw Sartre sitting happily in some squalid place near Marseilles, and protests: 'Sartre aimait l'inconfort.' Simone de Beauvoir herself, for that matter, can be considered no sybarite, judging by the account she gives of her way of living. By temperament intellectual and manly, taller than Sartre, and more imperious, she shrank not only from 'bourgeois marriage' but from the common domestic role of the female mate. She never made a home for herself and Sartre, who continued to a late age to live with his mother.

Apart from the success of his writings, Sartre was gratified in 1938 by an appointment to a lycée in Neuilly, which enabled him to

---

1. 'Mais il viendrait bien un moment où le livre serait écrit, serait derrière moi et je pense qu'un peu de sa clarté tomberait sur mon passé. A lors peut-être que je pourrais, à travers lui, me rappeler ma vie sans répugnance'. *La Nausée*, Paris, Gallimard, 1960, p. 222.

quit the uncongenial provinces for ever, and live thenceforth in
Paris. The war did not greatly disturb his routine. He went as a
meteorological clerk to the Maginot Line, where his duties were
confined to releasing balloons, to test the wind. He wrote to
Paulhan: 'This extremely pacific work (I feel that only carrier-
pigeon keepers, if the army still has any, can have a more gentle
and poetic employment) leaves me many hours of spare time, which
I am making use of to finish my novel.'[1]

This novel was *L'Age de raison*. During the victorious Nazi
advance of the summer 1940, Sartre was taken prisoner, but was
clever enough to persuade the Germans to repatriate him within a
year for 'health reasons'. At a medical examination in the camp he
showed his conspicuous wall-eye to the German doctor and claimed
that he suffered from *troubles de l'équilibre*. Once back in Paris,
Sartre participated with Merleau-Ponty, Cazin and other professors
in discussion which led to his becoming a Socialist. Sartre had good
friends also in the theatrical world. His first play *Les Mouches* was
staged during the Occupation in 1943 but enjoyed only a modest
success with the public. If the play is in some ways obscure, one
thing at least is clear: Sartre had abandoned the notion of 'salvation
through art' for something much closer to the notion of 'salvation
through action'. *Les Mouches* is a tragedy on the mock antique
model favoured by modern French dramatists: the hero Orestes
returns incognito to his native city of Argos, which he finds plagued
with flies and bowed down by a religion of national repentance: he
defies the orders of the Gods to quit the city, and remains to kill the
usurper King (his stepfather) and his treacherous mother, the
Queen. Then he goes away, proudly. The central argument of
the play turns on Orestes's refusal to accept the omnipotence of the
gods. Man is free, he tells Jupiter; therefore man must make his own
values. Orestes refuses to feel guilty for having killed the King and
Queen. He has obeyed his own moral law in doing so: and that is
the only moral law there is. He goes on to say that men are like
gods. Both are free: 'We are equally alone, and our anguish is the
same.'

1. Quoted by Simone de Beauvoir, *La Force de l'age*, Paris, Gallimard, 1960,
p. 440.

It must be said of this play that the moral law to which Orestes appeals is a very crude kind of moral law. Orestes kills to avenge his father's murder. And this is, at best, the feudal ethos of *El Cid*. Assuredly, it has been argued that *Les Mouches* is a 'Resistance' play, designed to uphold the right of the partisans to kill the German usurper and the French collaborator; but the objection to this reading is that Orestes does nothing for Argos apart from this one bloody deed, for which, in any case, he has a private motive. When he has done it, he simply leaves the city.

Nevertheless Sartre says some things in *Les Mouches* which deserve reflection. Sartre is surely right in ascribing the importance he does to human freedom or free will. To say that men have, in this sense, freedom is to say that they are not the puppets of the gods, or of the past, or of any other forces. They are free, independent, disconnected, isolated, 'on their own'. The future is entirely open. Admittedly Sartre says more than this: he associates the awareness of man's liberty with dread, anguish, vertigo. But this is only the emotional and sensational colour that Sartre adds to a picture which, in its essentials, is perfectly rational.

Another thing might perhaps be said in defence of Sartre. Although his philosophy rejects any absolute standard for the judgement of norms, it does have a method for distinguishing between one man's conduct and another. Sartre offers the criterion of sincerity, genuineness, or authenticity. The word 'sincerity' is not itself very prominent in his writings, but what does recur again and again is an expression which is its opposite, *la mauvaise foi* or bad faith. Sartre's argument is that since men are autonomous beings, creators of their own values, the one thing we can ask of them is that they should be true to their own values. For indeed if they don't bear witness to their principles in their actions, they cannot be said to *have* those principles at all. If they are not acted on the so-called principles are just words.

This point can be connected with Sartre's rejection of 'essentialism'. An essentialist can speak of a man who has a good nature, but who behaves badly. An existentialist cannot; in existentialist eyes, a man is the sum total of what he *does*. This idea is given forceful expression in Sartre's second play *Huis Clos* (1943). Once again the author makes effective use of the myths of the religion he claims to reject. *Huis Clos* is set in hell, albeit an unexpected kind of hell. It is a windowless room sparsely furnished in the style of the Second Empire. Three characters are introduced in turn. Each expects to find 'fires and brimstone and instruments of torture'. There are none. The three soon learn, however, they have not escaped punishment. They are to be their own tormentors. Each tortures the others: in a memorable phrase, 'Hell is other people'.

There are two women in the play, the older, a plain-speaking Lesbian named Inès (who ought, one feels, on Sartre's own morality to have been spared from hell because she is nothing if not authentic and sincere) is attracted to the younger woman, Estelle, who rejects her, and seeks to please the man, Garcin, who in turn desires to make a good impression on Inès, who despises him. Both Estelle and Garcin lie at first about the reason for their being damned, but eventually admit the truth. Garcin is a coward and in his bad faith he invokes the falsehood (as Sartre sees it) of essentialism to support his pretence that, although he has committed cowardly acts he has a brave soul or nature. Inès teaches him the painful existentialist message that a man is what he does, and no more. Garcin has no soul or essence to be brave. He is a coward because his deeds are cowardly.

One important fact about *Huis Clos* is that all the characters are dead. Some critics have called the play 'depressing', but at any rate it is not a lugubrious picture of life, because it is not a picture of life at all. The protagonists' lives are terminated, and so although they do not have essences, they do have complete biographies. Put in another way, they have no future; they can have no more projects. They are thus damned in the sense that the possibility of salvation is no longer open to them. If Garcin had been alive, there would be a continuing possibility of his ceasing to do cowardly deeds and beginning to do courageous deeds instead – thus of turning from a coward into a brave man. But as he is dead, it is too late. He can no longer redeem himself.

Sartre's decision to set *Huis Clos* in hell is therefore no mere theatrical device. The play is properly set in hell because its subject is damnation. In this way it explores the other side of the subject of salvation, which is examined in *La Nausée* and *Les Mouches*. In the same year as *Huis Clos* – 1943 – Sartre brought out his more substantial work of metaphysical and moral philosophy: *L'Etre et le Néant*. This book reached a public vastly wider than that which is usually interested in philosophical books and prepared the way for Sartre's enormous influence as an intellectual leader in France after the Liberation, and for the once fashionable but now almost forgotten, cult of existentialism by the bohemian youth of the Left Bank and elsewhere. Sartre does not in general accept Bishop Berkeley's doctrine that 'to exist is to be perceived', but he does adopt it, in a sense, in the case of the existence of human beings. According to his theory, it is only in a very indirect and complicated way that I can be said to exist as an object for myself. But, he maintains, I exist in a direct and simple way as an object for other people. They see me as part of the furniture of their external world. They observe my behaviour; I, seeing them see me, and knowing that they observe my behaviour, acquire through them a particular form of being which Sartre calls 'being-for-others'.

There is another form of being which Sartre distinguishes. A conscious being, a 'human reality', or thinking person has being 'for itself'. An object in the external world has being 'in itself'. The distinction between conscious beings and material objects is familiar enough in other philosophies, but in Sartre's system the distinction is built up into something altogether more elaborate and paradoxical. He requires us to acknowledge that whereas a being in itself *is*, a being for itself *is not*. Being in itself is as it appears to be. There is no difference, in this case, between appearance and reality. Being in itself has no 'inside' which is opposed to an outside. But being for itself is all inside. The world as it appears in reflection is a combination of the objective characteristics of the in itself – existence, solidity, quantity, movement: and the subjective contribution of the perceiving for itself.

The third form of existence is being 'for others'. 'If there is another,' Sartre writes, 'I have an outside. I have a nature.' Hegel also suggests that our self-consciousness exists only because it exists for another person. 'I need from the other person an acknowledgement of my being.' Sartre might be quoting from Hegel when he writes: 'the road of interiority passes through the other'. Sartre sums this up in this doctrine of the look or gaze. The gaze of the other person gives me existence for him, and thus mediately for myself. This relationship is reciprocal. To the other person I am, in turn, the other. My gaze gives *him* objective existence. Nor is this all. In so far as the look of another person turns me into an object it turns me into something 'solidified', something that has essence. So in a sense it *takes away my freedom*. Correspondingly, my look at the other takes away, in the same sense, his freedom. Thus we are presented with a kind of metaphysical struggle between two 'transcendences', each of which tries to 'out transcend' the other.

Sartre does not shrink from the implications of this theory. On the contrary, he advances without hesitation the conclusion that all relations between people are forms of conflict. He starts off by saying that it is the experience of *shame* which proves to us the existence of other people. For shame is a form of acknowledgement. I should not feel shame if there was nobody in the world to witness the action of which I am ashamed. In shame 'I recognize that I am as the other sees me. . . . I am ashamed of myself as I appear to the other.'

How do we behave in this situation? Sartre sees only two lines of conduct open to us. I may try to make myself the sort of object in the eyes of the other that I would wish to be. Or I may try to take away the other's freedom. Both lines of action are forms of conflict – the first finding its extreme expression in masochism, the second in sadism. Love Sartre describes as a project that can never be realized. For me to love you is nothing other than for me to try to make you love me. And since for you to love me is simply for you to try to make me love you, we are confronted by an infinite regress. We may engage in prolonged essays in mutual seduction, but we are doomed to eternal frustration. Because love is an impossible enterprise one may turn to the more desperate endeavour of masochism. But this again, Sartre says, cannot achieve its end. 'Masochism is an attempt not to fascinate the other by means of my objectivity, but to cause myself to be fascinated by my objectivity for others.' And masochism fails because the more the masochist tries to taste his objectivity, the more he becomes submerged in the consciousness of his subjectivity.

Sartre brackets love and masochism together because they are both attempts to assimilate the liberty of the other, while allowing the other to remain free. But there are types of relationship based on the wish to transform the other, to objectify him. One may attempt to avoid this by indifference: a shutting of one's eyes to the existence of others. This is a manifestation of bad faith. Its disadvantage is that it imposes a continuing strain, through the effort of keeping one's eyes shut; and also a constant uneasiness, because one knows that one is being watched by unseen eyes. Indifference fails: so we may attempt to get at the other person's freedom. Sartre calls one form of this 'desire', and characterizes it further as 'sexual' desire – for sexual desire, he says, is not just a wish for a body, it is a wish for that consciousness which gives meaning and unity to the body. And yet, he continues, desire (like love and masochism and indifference) cannot achieve its aim. For in the very satisfaction of desire 'is the death of desire'.

Hence the more desperate resort of sadism. In sadism, as in desire, the goal is to seize and make use of the other not only as object, but as pure incarnated transcendence. The sadist seeks to incarnate the other through violence. The sadist wants sexual relations to be non-reciprocal. He enjoys being a free appropriating power confronting a freedom captured by flesh. But sadism, again, is doomed to failure, because the freedom the sadist seeks to appropriate is out of reach. And the sadist discovers his error when his victim *looks* at him. For that look proves that the victim's transcendence has eluded him. Hatred is likewise doomed to permanent frustration. The aim of hatred is the extinction of the other, the hated one. And this is something that cannot be achieved, for although I can kill a man, terminate his life, *I cannot bring it about that he had never existed.* I cannot realize his non-being.

What are we to make of this forbidding catalogue of possible relations? Sartre does not claim to have given an exhaustive list, but he does maintain that these are the *fundamental* relationships, and that more complex patterns of conduct are mere 'enrichments' of these original attitudes. We always meet each other as 'competing transcendencies', and we shall never place ourselves, Sartre says, on a plain of equality when 'the recognition of the other's freedom would involve the recognition of our own freedom'.

Sartre is thus led to say that *'respect for the other's freedom is an empty word'*. He considers the idea that there are some concrete experiences in which we discover ourselves not at odds with others, but in community with them – the experience of *Mitsein* or togetherness. Such feelings, however, he dismisses as purely psychological or subjective. They reveal nothing about Being as such. It is altogether useless, he concludes, for man to try to escape from this dilemma: 'one must either transcend the Other, or allow oneself to be transcended by him. The essence of the relations between consciousness is not the *Mitsein*: it is conflict.'[1]

It is against this background of his theoretical works that one has, I think, to read Sartre's most ambitious work of fiction, *Les Chemins de la liberté*. The first part, *L'Age de raison* seeks to demonstrate the impossibility of community or togetherness. All the relations between the different characters verge on the sadistic or the masochistic. The volume which follows, *Le Sursis*, is an attempt to depict Munich week of 1938 as it impinges on a series of personalities, some real, some fictional. What it offers is a panorama of cowardice and bad faith, as everybody shirks his duty to nurse his self-interest. But the next volume, *La Mort dans l'âme* is characterized by a certain reversal of values. Even Mathieu, the 'anti-hero' of the earlier chapters dies the death of a certain kind of hero: Mathieu is called up for the army and in the summer of 1940, we find him at the front. His regiment is deserted by its officers as the Germans advance; and the men, who are demoralized and think only of going home, get drunk as they wait for the armistice. Then there appears in the village where Mathieu's unit is billeted a platoon from a first-class regiment of Chasseurs. There is no question of *these* men giving up easily or of their officers deserting them. Impressed by their soldierly qualities, Mathieu and a working-class friend persuade the Chasseurs to let them join them on the church tower, where they are making a last stand against the enemy.

Up in the tower, doomed to be destroyed by the Germans, the ineffectual Mathieu has a last hour of spectacular action:

1. *L'Etre et le néant*, Paris, Gallimard, 1943, p. 502; *Being and Nothingness*, trans. Hazel Barnes, London, Methuen, New York, Random House, 1957, p. 429.

He made his way to the parapet and stood there firing. This was revenge on a big scale. Each one of his shots avenged some ancient scruple. 'One for Lola, whom I dared not rob; one for Marcelle, whom I ought to have left in the lurch; one for Odette, whom I didn't want to kiss. This for the books I never dared to write, this for the journeys I never made, this for anybody in general whom I wanted to hate and tried to understand.' He fired, and the tables of the Law crashed about him. Thou Shalt Love Thy Neighbour as Thyself – bang! in that bugger's face; Thou Shalt Not Kill – bang! at that scarecrow opposite. He was firing on his fellow men, on Virtue, on the whole world. Liberty is Terror. The *mairie* was ablaze, his head was ablaze. Bullets were whining round him free in the air. 'The world is going up in smoke and me with it . . .'

Mathieu went on firing. He fired. He was cleansed. He was all-powerful; He was free.[1]

The whole atmosphere of this section of the novel is exceedingly romantic. The cowardice of those who do not want to fight is seen through stern, contemptuous eyes. The military virtues of the Chasseurs are plainly held up for admiration, and in Mathieu's death there is a slightly naïve touch of a Hollywood war film. However, as Sartre's shrewd critic Philip Thody has pointed out, Mathieu is not meant to be a 'cad who made good'; he is meant to be 'the incarnation of what Hegel called "terrorist liberty" '.

And this idea of 'terrorist liberty' is one which plays a very large part in Sartre's later thought. Once 'converted to Marxism', according to his own account, he ceased to be dominated by the conception of freedom as a metaphysical or as a moral category, and instead became deeply concerned with freedom as a political category. The kind of 'terrorist liberty' expressed in Mathieu's sensational death was perhaps originally intended by Sartre to be the final irony in Mathieu's biography. But Sartre's attitude turned out to be very much less straightforward. He was coming more and more to regard 'terrorist liberty' as the noblest expression of political freedom that man can achieve.

His decision to abandon the fourth volume of *Les Chemins de la liberté* is thus in several ways significant. Once his 'anti-hero' had

1. *Iron in the Soul*, trans. G. Hopkins, London, Hamish Hamilton, 1950, p. 193.

become a 'hero', there did not seem any more to be said about him. Besides after having explored several wrong 'roads to freedom', Sartre did not feel that the novel as such was the appropriate literary medium for the demonstration of the right 'road to freedom'.

Since he abandoned this novel sequence in 1949, Sartre has written no fiction whatever. Politics, or more precisely socialism has become his chief, his all-pervasive concern. The phrase 'committed literature' meant, as he originally defined it, literature committed to any genuinely moral view of life, no matter what. Indeed it could not be otherwise on the existentialist principle that every man must be the maker of his own values. But by some obscure shuffling of the cards, Sartre began to use the phrase 'committed literature' to mean 'literature committed to socialism' as if no other commitment could possibly be genuine. This curious sleight of hand can be seen at work if one compares the arguments of Sartre's two books of 'psychoanalytic' literary criticism, *Baudelaire* (1947) and *Saint Genet* (1953). Sartre claims in the first book that Baudelaire 'went wrong' at the age of seven, when, after his mother's remarriage, he deceived himself into believing that it was his destiny to be 'for ever alone'. Baudelaire thereafter repudiated any social obligations and cultivated a form of dandyism and diabolism which was, in effect, bourgeois and reactionary. Genet, whose life Sartre analyses by the same methods, also made a decisive choice at an early age. Genet was a bastard (Baudelaire, like Sartre himself, being a mere orphan, or 'false bastard', in the Sartrian terminology), and Genet was caught stealing things. Genet heard himself called 'the Thief' and henceforth decided to *be* what he heard himself called. He became a dedicated criminal. Now, the striking thing is that whereas Sartre attacks Baudelaire for choosing to be what he believed himself destined to be, he praises Genet for choosing to be what he heard himself called, indeed, he canonizes him. But what is the difference between these two cases? Morally, one must say, very little. The real difference is political. Genet was an enemy of the bourgeoisie, whereas Baudelaire ended on the side of the reactionaries. This, and this alone, is why Sartre exalts the one, and damns the other. But Sartre cannot bring himself to say this in so many words. He pretends that his case against Baudelaire turns on the choice the poet made (at the age of seven) 'in bad faith' to succumb to his destiny, when there is no such thing as destiny. But he makes no similar accusations against Genet. The result is bad criticism, whether moral or literary.

Sartre, converted, as he put it, to Marxism, was for years tormented by one question: should he or should he not join the Communist Party? He supported its politics, on the whole, until the later 1960s: but he could not bring himself to stomach its philosophy. So he never joined the Party, but became a sort of irritable fellow traveller, criticizing the Party from time to time, but defending it fiercely when anyone else attacked it.

In February 1963 Sartre said: 'If I were an Italian I would join the Italian Communist Party.'[1] This was widely assumed to mean that Sartre preferred the more tolerant and less dogmatic characteristics of the Italian, as opposed to the French C.P. But it did not mean that he wanted a more liberal or democratic type of communism. On the contrary he wanted a more extreme and revolutionary kind. He was to the left of the Communists: and when, after the death of Stalin, most Communist Parties of the world became more moderate and more concerned with coexistence, Sartre's patience with official Communism was sorely tried and finally exhausted.

In his journal *Les Temps Modernes*, in 1966, Sartre urged the Russians to intervene in the Vietnam war against the Americans: to use the Soviet artillery against the American seventh fleet, even at the risk of a Third World War: 'Deliberately to run the risk of war today: such is the surest way of avoiding having to choose tomorrow between the reality of an imposed war and the destruction one after the other of all the revolutionary states and movements of Asia and elsewhere.'[2] Khrushchev's doctrine of peaceful coexistence did not appeal to Sartre. 'Peaceful coexistence', he wrote in 1966, 'serves only the U.S.A.'[3]

1. Quoted by François Bondy, 'Jean-Paul Sartre', in Cranston, ed. *The New Left*, London, The Bodley Head, New York, The Library Press, 1971, p. 66.
2. *Les Temps Modernes*, no. 243, Aug. 1966, p. 196.
3. *Le Nouvel Observateur*, 30 Nov. 1966, p. 14.

The students' revolt and the general strike in France in May 1968 seemed to him to offer at last the real possibility of revolution. When the revolution did not take place, Sartre blamed the French Communist Party for having sabotaged the cause. For what the French C.P. had done in the crisis of May 1968 was to extract from the frightened employers new wage settlements favourable to the workers. Thus, according to Sartre, the French C.P. instead of exploiting a golden opportunity for revolution, had helped to rescue capitalism by reforming it, and so paved the way for the triumphant return of the Gaullist government. This, for Sartre, marked the end of his respect for the French C.P.

His belief that reformism was the enemy of revolution he had made clear enough in his controversy with Camus and others in the 1950s. When he came to feel that the entire working class of Western Europe was permeated with reformist sentiment, Sartre began to despair of Europe altogether. For hope he looked to China and Cuba, and to a new proletariat composed of the poor inhabitants of the undeveloped world. A young friend of his, a black Martinquais named Frantz Fanon, wrote a book with the arresting title *Les Damnés de la terre*, which suggested that the wretched of the earth in the Third World might enact the revolutionary role assigned by Marx to the industrialized working class.

Fanon in his text argued the case for a violent revolution against colonialism. Sartre wrote a preface for the book which pleaded for violence with even more fervour than did Fanon himself, and perhaps to some extent distorted the emphasis of Fanon's argument by the excited language used in praise of violence. Sartre's words are:

The native cures himself of his colonial neurosis by thrusting out the settler through force of arms. When his rage boils over he rediscovers his lost innocence and he comes to know himself in the act of creating himself . . . to shoot down a European is to kill two birds with one stone, to destroy an oppressor and the man he oppresses at the same time.[1]

This last epigram embodies a thought which is Sartre's rather than Fanon's. Fanon himself writes of violence in more Sorelian

1. *The Wretched of the Earth*, trans. C. Farrington, London and Baltimore Penguin Books, 1967.

terms, not as killing white men, but as impassioned participation in a struggle for liberty. Sartre himself, as we have noticed, has a less poetic conception of violence. His violence is the voice of the gun.

How far is Sartre the Marxist that he claims to be? For an answer to this we must look to the most substantial theoretical works of his later years, the *Critique de la raison dialectique*, published in 1960, and his essay on *Flaubert*, published in 1971. Both these works are long, diffuse, replete with the technical language, and sometimes obscure. No one has as yet translated them into English. They exact some effort on the part of the reader: but the effort is rewarded. The *Critique de la raison dialectique* has an ambitious title, if only because of the obvious reference to Kant's *Kritik der reinen Vernunft*. And indeed Sartre sees himself as doing something analogous to Kant. Where Kant, as Sartre supposes, was making a synthesis of empiricism and rationalism, Sartre is attempting to make a synthesis of existentialism and Marxism. In a prefatory essay, *Question de méthode*, Sartre explains that he has set out to revitalize and modernize Marxism by giving it a new method. In the main body of the *Critique* he shows how this modernized or existentialized Marxism unfolds itself in a new *anthropologie* (in Kant's sense of that word), that is to say, in a philosophical theory of man and society.

Sartre's approach to the subject is not, as he explains, purely academic. His *Question de méthode* appeared originally in a Polish journal in 1957, when 'destalinization' first became the order of the day, and the theory is consciously put forward as a destalinized philosophy for bewildered Communist intellectuals, and as a basis for reunion between such intellectuals and those of the Left who were outside the Party: that is to say, as something to fill minds left painfully empty by Moscow's repudiation of Stalin's teaching, and as a theoretical foundation for a new united front against the bourgeoisie. This public-spirited purpose in no way detracts from the academic interest of the *Critique*; many of the best political theorists have had some such further motive; the philosopher and the polemicist are often the same man.

Sartre begins by paying the most lavish tributes to Marxism

4*

and making the most modest claims for existentialism. Indeed he says that whereas Marxism is one of the main philosophies of the modern world, existentialism is not even a genuine philosophy at all. Existentialism is merely an 'ideology'. But he does not use the word *ideology* in Marx's sense. He provides his own Sartrian definition both of that word and of the word *philosophy*. Philosophies, according to Sartre, are the great creative systems of thought which dominate certain 'moments' or periods of history, systems which cannot be got beyond (*dépassé*) until history itself has moved on to another stage. Thus in the seventeenth century, the philosophical 'moment' was that of Descartes and Locke; at the end of the eighteenth and the beginning of the nineteenth century, it was the 'moment' of Kant and Hegel; our own age is that of Marx. No philosophy could go beyond Descartes and Locke in their time, or Kant and Hegel in theirs; and no philosophy can go beyond Marx today. We are compelled, Sartre says, to think in Marxist terms.

Not content with this exalting Marxism, Sartre is at pains to diminish existentialism, the mere ideology. Ideologies, in this Sartrian sense, are little systems which live on the edge of the great systems of thought, and which 'exploit the domain' of the genuine philosophies. Since the present century falls within the Marxist epoch, existentialism 'exploits the domain of Marxism'. Existentialism, then, is 'a parasitic system which lives on the margin of a Knowledge to which it was at first opposed, but into which it seeks now to integrate itself'.[1]

This is a decidedly original perspective. There is also something audacious about the proposal that existentialism should 'integrate itself' into Marxism, for no two systems of thought could be more dissimilar. Two things, at least, would seem to offer insuperable obstacles to any fusion. First, existentialists believe in free will, libertarianism, indeterminism; and Sartre in particular has always put great emphasis on this. No theme is more marked and recurrent in all his work than that man is 'condemned to be free'. Marx, on the other hand, belongs to that tradition of philosophy which would banish the free will problem altogether. Freedom, for Marx, is in Hegel's words, 'recognition of necessity'. Marx holds first that all

1. Sartre, *Critique de la raison dialectique*, Paris, Gallimard, p. 18.

history is shaped and determined by the relations of production according to certain laws and secondly, that men can master their destiny in so far as they understand those laws and consciously direct their action in accordance with them. Thus Marx thinks he is entitled to believe equally in both freedom and determination. For Sartre, on the other hand, determinism is not only false, it is a form of *mauvaise foi*, or culpable self-deception, by means of which certain people evade their moral responsibility.

Next, there is the matter of individualism. Existentialists lay great stress on the isolation, the solitude, the 'abandonment' of the individual; and no existentialist writer has stressed this more than Sartre, from his earliest novel *La Nausée* to his latest play *Les Séquestrés d'Altona*. But Marxism regards individualism as a 'delusion of theory' and holds that man's true nature is a social one.

Sartre does not shirk these contradictions. He believes they can be resolved. He suggests that the trouble lies in the fact that Marxism – orthodox Marxism – has become out-of-date, hidebound, dogmatic; and has lost its touch with humanity. This is where existentialism can help to renovate it – by 'humanizing' Marxism. Sartre goes on to make this curious prediction:

> From the day that Marxist research takes on a human dimension (that is to say, the existential project), as the basis of its sociological knowledge, existentialism will no longer have a reason for being – absorbed, transcended and conserved by the totalising movement of philosophy, it will cease to be one particular enquiry, and become the basis of all enquiry.[1]

Sartre insists that his quarrel is with the Marxists and not with Marx; indeed he gives an interpretation of Marx's essay on the 'Eighteenth Brumaire' which suggests that Marx himself, in his most inspired moments, was an existentialist without realizing it. Sartre's complaint about the Marxists is that they are lazy. Sometimes they are too metaphysical and sometimes too positivistic. Their thinking is old-fashioned, and often it is not thinking at all, but blind assent to authority.

Many of Sartre's criticisms of the orthodox Marxists hit the nail on the head. He shows, for example, how shallow is the judgement

1. Ibid., p. 111.

of those Marxist literary critics who discuss Valéry as a 'petit bourgeois intellectual'. Sartre agrees: Valéry *is* a petit bourgeois intellectual, but the important point is that 'not every petit bourgeois intellectual is a Valéry'. Sartre also demonstrates the absurdity of the Marxist critical habit of bundling together such diverse writers as Proust, Joyce, Bergson, and Gide as 'subjective'; he shows that this category of the subjective is of no use to criticism; it is not drawn from experience; it is not based on the study and observation of real men.

'Lazy Marxists', Sartre says, reveal their laziness not only in their unreflective use of categories but in their tendency to constitute the real *a priori*. Just as Communist Party politicians use these methods to prove that what has happened had to happen, so Marxist intellectuals use it to prove that everything is what it was bound to be. And this, Sartre shrewdly observes, is a method of 'exposition' from which one learns nothing. It is tautologous; it cannot teach us anything, because it knows in advance what it is going to find out. Hence Sartre's belief in the need for giving Marxism a new method.

He describes this method which existentialism offers Marxism as 'heuristic'; that is to say, it is a method serving to discover truth; it is also 'dialectic'. Sartre asserts that whereas the lazy Marxist when confronted with any problem immediately refers to abstract principles, his own new method works by no other means than that of 'cross reference' (the *va-et-vient*) within the flux and movement of the real world. For example, Sartre's method would seek to explain the biography of individuals like Flaubert or Robespierre by an equally deep study of the epoch which shapes the individual and of the individual who shapes the epoch. He calls it the Progressive-Regressive method. It is progressive because it seeks part of the explanation in the aims of conscious beings; and it is regressive because it looks at the conditions in which each conscious being pursues his objectives. People have to be understood both in terms of their own aims and in the light of the circumstances in which they formulate and seek to realize their aims.

Sartre gives an interesting example of what he has in mind in discussing the case of Flaubert. Sartre is as quick as any lazy Marxist to classify and castigate Flaubert as a petit bourgeois. But this is only the beginning. The important thing about Flaubert, for Sartre, is not that his class was petit bourgeois but what he did to rise above that condition. Flaubert, in Sartre's words, 'threw himself across the several fields of possibility towards the alienated objectivation of himself, creating himself ineluctably and indissolubly as the author of *Madame Bovary* and as the petit bourgeois that he refused to be'.[1]

Flaubert's career is thus seen as instance of the project (*le projet*). This is a characteristically existentialist concept and one of which Sartre has often made use. It figures prominently in the most substantial work of his earlier years, and still perhaps his masterpiece, *L'Etre et le néant* (1943), where the project is defined as the way in which a person chooses his mode of life and creates himself in action. The design according to which we make ourselves is our project. Of Flaubert's project, creating himself as an objective being in the shape of an author, or more precisely as *the* author of *Madame Bovary* and other novels, Sartre writes:

This project has a *meaning*. It is not a simple negativity, the flight (from the petty bourgeois predicament); but rather through it, the man aims at the production of himself in the world as a certain objective totality. It is not the pure and simple abstract choice to write that makes the nature of Flaubert, but the choice to write in a certain fashion so as to manifest himself in the world in a certain way – in a word, it is the particular meaning that he gives (in the framework of contemporary ideology) to literature as the negation of his original condition, and as the objective resolution of his contradictions.[2]

A man 'defines himself' by his project. We make ourselves what we are by what we do. Sartre has had something to say about this in several of his earlier books. For example Garcin, in *Huis Clos*, could have done better deeds and died a hero. Flaubert equally could have made a worse choice, and lived in idleness as a *rentier*, and then he would not have been *the* Flaubert we know, the author of *Madame Bovary*. In *L'Etre et le néant*, the notion of the project is bound up with existence; and here again, in the *Critique*, Sartre speaks of the project as a kind of 'uprooting of oneself towards existence'; and by

1. Ibid., p. 93.
2. Ibid.

existence, he adds, 'we do not understand a stable substance, which abides in itself, but a perpetual disequilibrium, an uprooting of the whole body. And this drive towards objectivation takes different forms in different individuals as each projects himself forward through a field of possibilities – of which he realizes some to the exclusion of others. We existentialists call this Choice, or Liberty.'[1]

Manifestly Sartre has retained the libertarian principle of existentialism and by no means assimilated the Marxist theory of necessity. So in spite of all that he said at the beginning about Marxism being the true philosophy and existentialism being a mere ideology, it is obvious that an essential part of the so-called integration between the two will have to be the surrender by the Marxist, and not by the existentialist, of one fundamental belief. To modify the shock of this demand, Sartre invokes the aid of the Marxist concept of *Praxis*. This word is often used by Marx and his followers, though not always in the same sense. At different places in Marxist writings, *Praxis* appears to mean (1) the common sense that stands opposed to speculation, (2) the process of acting, as opposed to meditation, by which understanding is acquired, (3) empirical, scientific, or industrial work. Now Sartre, with some adroitness, has taken this somewhat ambiguous Marxist notion of *Praxis* and made it more or less identical with the existentialist notion of the project. In other words, Sartre uses this idea of *Praxis* as a means of introjecting his own notion of project into Marxism. The notion of project, as we have seen from the quotation above, is a libertarian one. Therefore if the notion of *Praxis* could be interpreted as meaning what 'project' means, and the Marxist admits to believing in *Praxis*, then the Marxist might be shown to believe in free will without knowing it. Hence if the concepts of project and *Praxis* are to be united, it is the Marxist, and not the existentialist, who is going to have to make a radical revision of his categories.

We may next consider the other subject on which existentialism and Marxism are notoriously at variance: individualism. Existentialism as it is commonly understood, and certainly as it is expounded by Sartre, entails an extreme form of individualism, whereas Marxism has no more conspicuous feature than its rejection of

1. Ibid., p. 95.

individualism – its belief that man must be seen in terms of the social whole or common humanity. Sartre has attempted to resolve this antithesis by putting forward in his *Critique* a theory of society which he claims to be both Marxist and existentialist. How far can he be said to have succeeded?

Once again Sartre makes free use of the kind of technical language which is favoured by Marxists. First, he invokes the notion of alienation. But Sartre, as we shall see, has a different theory of alienation from that of Marx. Whereas Marx saw alienation as the result of the exploitation of one man by another, Sartre sees alienation as a feature of the human predicament. Indeed Sartre's notion of alienation cannot be understood in purely Marxist terms. The words Sartre shares with Marx are words they have both rifled from Hegel. Sartre's theory of alienation is an existentialized Hegelian concept, not an existentialized Marxist concept. His alienation, already explained in *L'Etre et le néant*, is *metaphysical*. Nevertheless he does not forget that his subject here is *l'anthropologie* as opposed to *l'ontologie*; and that a fresh, and so to speak, specifically socio-logical reason has to be given for what he has always regarded as the fundamental characteristic of human relations – mutual antagonism.

This theory is developed in the most striking, if also the most intricate, sections of the *Critique*. The principle Sartre introduces at this point is that of shortage, or *scarcity*. Sartre says that all human history – at any rate, all human history hitherto – has been a history of shortage and of a bitter struggle against shortage. There is not enough in this world to go around, and there never has been. And it is this *scarcity*, according to the *Critique*, which makes human rela-tionships intelligible. Scarcity is the key to understanding the atti-tude of men to one another and to understanding the social structures men have built up during their life on earth. Scarcity, says Sartre, both unites and divides us. It unites us because it is only by united efforts that we are able to struggle at all successfully against scarcity; it divides us because each one of us knows that it is only the existence of others which prevents there being abundance for oneself.

Scarcity then is 'the motor of history'. No man can eliminate scarcity altogether. In this sense, men are powerless or impotent. The best that any man can do is to try to overcome scarcity by collaboration with others. But such collaboration is itself paradoxical, for each of the collaborators knows that it is the existence in the world of others that makes scarcity. I am a rival to you, and you are a rival to me. When I work together with others to struggle against scarcity, I am working with those whose existence makes that work necessary; and by my work I nourish my competitors and rivals. Scarcity, then, not only shapes our attitude to the natural world, it shapes our attitude to our neighbours. Scarcity makes us all rivals, yet compels us to collaborate with our rivals; for being impotent alone, we can only act effectively against scarcity by the division of labour and other such joint endeavours.

Nature, however, is 'inert' and indifferent to human welfare. The world we inhabit is in part the world of nature and in part a world that has been made by our forebears in the course of their long struggle against scarcity. Sartre calls it the world of the *Practico-Inert*. The world is the world of *Praxis* in so far as it is a world shaped by the work and projects of its past and present inhabitants. This is the world to the extent that it is man-made. But the world is also the passive, or inert, world of nature on which man has had to work. Ironically, many of the things that men have done with the aim of making the world more bearable have had the effect not of improving but of worsening the world. Sartre gives the example of Chinese peasants cutting down wood to make fires and to build houses, and doing this on so large a scale, that they effectively deforest their land, and so expose themselves to the hazards and disasters of constant floods. Men are tormented by their own inventions in the world of the Practico-Inert.

Thus, in a hostile universe, defined by scarcity, man becomes the enemy of man. In a typically Sartrian phrase, man becomes anti-man, *le contre-homme*. And in a paragraph which is dramatic enough to be a speech in one of his plays, Sartre writes:[1]

Nothing indeed – neither wild beasts nor microbes – could be more terrible for man than this intelligent, flesh-eating, cruel species, which knows how to follow and outwit the human intelligence and of which the aim is precisely the destruction of man. This species is manifestly our own, as each of us sees it, in the Other, in the context of scarcity.

1. Ibid., p. 208.

The conflicts – or relationships of antagonism – between man and man are thus given an *economic* explanation in the *Critique*. Antagonism is negative reciprocity; but that negation is itself negated in the collaboration between neighbours which is necessary to overcome scarcity. Such is Sartre's 'dialectical' theory of the origin of society. He distinguishes two forms of social structure: one he calls the *series*, the other the *group*. The two are significantly different. A series is a collection of people who are united only by external proximity. It does not exist as a whole 'inside' any of its members. The example Sartre gives of a series is a queue or line at a bus stop. This is a collection or gathering of people that can be observed. You can look at it, count the number of people in it. Everyone is there for the 'same' purpose; but they do not have a *common* or collective purpose. No one is interested in the others. Indeed, each member of the queue is a rival of the others. Because of the scarcity of seats in the bus, each wishes the others were not there. Each is superfluous, each is one too many. But because everyone *knows* that he also is one too many to the others, just as each of the others is one too many to him, all agree to take it in turn to get on the bus when the bus comes. They form an orderly series to avoid a fight or war on the platform of the bus. The forming of an orderly series like a queue waiting for a bus is thus a negative reciprocal relationship which is the negation of antagonism, it is the negation of itself.

The people in the queue form a plurality of solitudes. Sartre maintains that the whole social life of mankind is permeated by series of this kind. A city is a series of series. The bourgeoisie is a series, each member respecting the solitude of the others. But in human society, there is another kind of collection or gathering which Sartre recognizes; and this is what he calls the *group*. A group is a recollection of people who, unlike those in a series, *do* have a common objective or end. A football team is the example he gives. The difference between a group and series is inward. What makes a group is the fact that each member has committed himself to act as a member of that group. The group is held together, and therefore constituted, by commitment. Each member, as Sartre puts it, has converted his own individual *Praxis* to a common or social *Praxis*. The working class becomes a group when its members commit themselves to socialism. A group can accomplish things, whereas a series is impotent, since each member pursues only his own *Praxis*. And indeed it is precisely *because* the series is impotent that the group is constituted in the first place. The origin of the group, Sartre suggests, can be summed up in the discovery that 'we must either live by working together, or die by fighting each other'.

Scarcity again is the driving force, since it is scarcity, and scarcity alone, which makes men work together for a common end. Scarcity is thus seen as the origin of the group. And in developing this thought, Sartre introduces three colourful notions: the pledge (*le serment*), violence, and Terror. Sartre explains that the group comes into being when each individual gives his pledge to become a member of the group and not to defect from or betray the group. A group is thus defined as a *pledged* group. But the pledge must be enforced, and the members must be assured that it will be enforced. This is where violence and Terror come in. It is fear which drives men to form groups in the first place, and it is fear that must keep them in these groups. The institutionalized violence and threat of violence which frightens men into remaining in their groups is Terror. Indeed the pledge itself, says Sartre, is an invitation for violence to be used against oneself if one breaks one's own word; and the existence of Terror is an assurance that violence will be used equally against any other member of the group who tries to break his pledge.

All groups, says Sartre, are in constant danger of dissolving into seriality. Everyone is conscious of the threat of dispersion in himself and in others. Hence Sartre can say that 'Terror is the statutory guarantee, freely called for, that none shall fall back into seriality'. Terror indeed is more than this: it is 'mortal solicitude', for it is thanks to Terror that man becomes a social being, created such by himself and by others. Terror is the violence that negates violence. Terror indeed is fraternity. For Terror is the guarantee that my neighbour will stay my brother; it binds my neighbour to me by the threat of the violence it will use against him if he dares to be 'unbrotherly'.

The most important example of a group which Sartre gives is the state. The state, he says, 'is a group which reconstitutes itself incessantly, and modifies its composition by a partial renewal – discontinuous or continuous – of its members'.[1] Sartre argues that the group in fusion throws up leaders; later the group perpetuates itself by founding institutions. This is the basis of sovereignty. Authority is connected with Terror in the sense that the sovereign is the man who is authorized to exercise Terror. In a serial society, I obey because I have to obey. But in a state I obey myself because it is I, by my pledge, who have merged myself in the group and authorized the sovereign to command. Sartre does not, of course, fancy that every member of a state has actually given his pledge personally; he has been pledged *by proxy*; but the pledge is no less a pledge.

Now, Terror is not only fraternity; it is also liberty. For I freely merge my individual project in the common project when I pledge myself (or am pledged by proxy) to the state; and when the sovereign, fortified by Terror, commands me on behalf of the state, he is giving me back my freedom.

Such, in summary terms, is Sartre's theory of social structures. How far can it be considered a Marxist theory? There is not much doubt that it is a thoroughly *Sartrian* theory, one which harmonizes completely with the theory of human relationships put forward in *L'Etre et le néant*, and summed up by a character in his play *Huis Clos* with the remark 'hell is other people'. This theory is, briefly, the following: If I speak, I objectify myself in words. Those words, once uttered and heard by other people, become *things* in the external world. Other people can hear them, think about them, talk about them. My words are part of the furniture of *their* world. Once I have spoken them they are no longer, strictly speaking, mine. I can no longer control them. This is what leads Sartre to say that in communicating with other people, or indeed even in being seen and heard by other people, I lose part of my self to other People. I cease to be a Self to myself and become an Other to another. At the same time, you become an Other to me. It is the Other Person, the Witness, who makes each of us an object in the universe – and to that extent robs each of us of our complete freedom. The word Sartre uses for this otherness is *alterity* (*alterité*).

This theory of alterity (which owes much to Hegel) Sartre

1. Ibid., p. 610.

developed fairly fully in that earlier exposition of existentialism, *L'Etre et le néant*, where he argued that relations between people are inevitably subject to mutual tensions because each individual, acting towards others as an objectifying Other, robs others of their liberty. This is what leads Sartre in *L'Etre et le néant* to say that all relations between men are forms of metaphysical conflict, each individual trying to outtranscend the other, each robbing the other of the other's freedom by objectifying him as a *thing* in the world, and each trying to defend his own freedom from being thus objectified. Sartre's conclusion in *L'Etre et le néant* is that the only possible relations between people are those which tend towards the sadistic and those which tend towards the masochistic. Togetherness, harmony, love, *Mitsein* being impossible, all relationships between men are relationships of conflict. In the *Critique*, Sartre gives a new reason for this conflict; but the conclusion is the same. He still maintains that each individual is at war with all the others; and even though he now speaks of some groups being formed, these groups are held together only by the pledge and Terror; they are in constant danger of relapsing in the individualistic condition of the series. Just as love, togetherness, friendship is rejected in *L'Etre et le néant*, so here is any Aristotelian notion of man being social by nature.

And precisely because this social and political theory of Sartre is so close to his own earlier teaching, it is all the further removed from Marxism. First, Marxism, though ambiguous in many ways, is unambiguous in its rejection of the picture of mankind as divided into individualistic and competing atoms. Marxism believes in community or social unity as the natural condition of man, and regards class antagonisms as the product of exploitation. Therefore all this talk about pledges and political societies being held together by pledges is the antithesis of Marxism. Secondly, Sartre's theory of scarcity has nothing in common with Marxist economics, which is, indeed, directly opposed to the scarcity theory as put forward by Malthus and other economists of the classical school who followed Hume. Marx says that men lived originally together in a state of primitive communism; then with the invention of things like iron tools and machinery, some men learned to exploit others. Expropriation reduced the dispossessed to a condition of penurious slavery; the exploiters stole from the slaves the difference between what they produced and what was needed to keep the slaves alive. And this, as Marx said, is a theory of *surplus*, not a theory of scarcity. The scarcity is the result of exploitation, not a characteristic of nature.

So Sartre's aim of producing a modernized Marxism can hardly be said to have been achieved. Indeed one has the impression in reading Sartre's *Critique*, that Sartre himself has forgotten his original intention. His early talk about Marxism being the great philosophy and existentialism being the mere ideology gives way to increasingly bold assertions about the metaphysical status of his own system. Already by page 153, Sartre says he is going 'to establish *a priori*' (and not as the Marxists think of doing, *a posteriori*) 'the heuristic value of the dialectic method'. He goes on to explain that starting with the discovery of the existential validity of the dialectical reason, he proposes to show that 'the dialectical method will be efficacious as a method in so far as it will become permanently *necessary* as a law of intelligibility and as the rational structure of *being*'.[1]

Sartre is thus making for his theory higher claims than Marx makes for his; Sartre is out, as he puts it, 'to establish an order of certitudes'. And this is something more than Sartre allowed in his preliminary essay, *Question de méthode*, to Descartes, Locke, Kant, Hegel, *or* Marx; all these 'great philosophies' had validity only within the context of their historical periods and as expressions of the aspiration of the rising class of the time. Sartre's own system, however, is going to be *necessarily* true, a law of the rational structure of *being*. So much for existentialism as a 'mere ideology'.

Sartre's 'restatement' of Marxism is certainly more sophisticated than the original thing, but how far can it be considered a 'modernization'? One striking feature of the theory is that it moves from nineteenth-century philosophy not forward to that of the twentieth, but back to that of the eighteenth and even seventeenth centuries. This is not only a question of language, although Sartre's talk of 'Liberty' as 'Terror' and 'Terror' as 'Fraternity' might come straight from a

1. Ibid., p 128.

speech by Robespierre. It is the basic elements of the theory which belong to pre-Hegelian thought. For Sartre is putting forward a doctrine of social covenant which is almost identical with that of the seventeenth-century English philosopher Thomas Hobbes. Sartre then adds to Hobbes's doctrine something which comes directly from one of Hobbes's critics, namely the theory of scarcity put forward by the eighteenth-century Scotsman David Hume.

Hobbes's word is not *violence*, it is *war*; he does not speak of a 'pledge', but a 'covenant'; he does not speak of 'Terror', but of a sovereign who keeps peace between men by 'holding them all in *awe*'. The words are slightly different, but the theory is uncannily the same. Neither Hobbes nor Sartre offers what is, strictly speaking, a social contract theory of the kind one finds in Locke or Rousseau, but both Hobbes and Sartre hold promise-and-force theories. And although Sartre's theory of sovereignty is a little more elaborate, perhaps, than Hobbes's, Sartre says exactly what Hobbes says about fear being the basis of political society and about the sovereign being *authorized* by the people to do whatever he decides to do, and so giving them back their freedom when he commands them to act as he wills. And just as Hobbes is haunted by fear of political society relapsing into the intolerable condition of the state of nature where no man is safe, Sartre gives grim warnings about the danger of the group's relapsing into an intolerable condition of seriality. Sartre writes:

The group is not a metaphysical reality, but a certain practical relationship between men towards a shared objective and among themselves. If certain circumstances of the struggle lead to a disbanding, and if this is not followed by a regroupment, the group is dead, the contagious panic re-establishes the dominion of the Practico-Inert – *voilà tout*.[1]

Voilà everything indeed – and how extraordinarily Hobbesian everything looks. What does not look Hobbesian looks Humian. The theory that scarcity lies at the origin of society (though anticipated in some of the unpublished work of Locke) was first elaborated by Hume in the Third Book of his *Treatise of Human Nature*, in this memorable passage:

1. Ibid., p. 427n.

Of all the animals with which this globe is peopled, there is none towards whom nature seems, at first sight, to have exercised more cruelty than towards man, in the numberless wants and necessities with which she has loaded him, and in the slender means which she affords to the relieving of these necessities. . . . It is by society alone he is able to supply his defects, and raise himself up to an equality with his fellow-creatures and even acquire a superiority above them. . . . When every individual person labours apart and only for himself, his force is too small to execute any considerable work; his labour being employed in supplying all his different necessities, he never attains a perfection in any particular art; and as his force and success are not at all times equal, the least failure in either of these particulars must be attended with inevitable ruin and misery. Society provides a remedy for these *three* inconveniences.[1]

Hume argues that society which comes into being because of scarcity entails what he calls a 'convention' being entered into by all its members, but he denies that this convention is 'of the nature of a promise'; society arises only 'from a general sense of the common interest'. Hume was attacking, among other sorts of promise, the Hobbesian notion of the 'covenant'; but Sartre, though he takes the Humian notion of scarcity, has to restore the Hobbesian notion of promise because, like Hobbes, Sartre puts great emphasis on the idea of *war* between men as part of their natural condition; in the world of the Practico-Inert for Sartre, as in the state of nature for Hobbes, there is no 'general sense of the common interest', for all men are enemies and rivals.

Are we to conclude that there are no elements of Marxism in Sartre's theory? That, I think, would be an unjustified conclusion. But the Marxist elements are all peripheral; and one is much more conscious of them in Sartre's literary and journalistic writings than in the pages of the *Critique*.

However, in the light of his political attitudes, Sartre's *anthropologie* as expounded in the *Critique* may be seen to have a personal utility for the author, however unacceptable it may be to others. For this new theory enables Sartre to defend the superiority of socialist over bourgeois societies in terms of the superiority of the group over the series. It also enables him to defend the Terror exercised by such

1. David Hume, *Treatise*, book III, part ii, section 2.

institutions as the Stalinist state as a violence that is *authorized* by those who are pledged and as a violence that is needed to prevent the dissolution of the group into seriality. Thus Sartre has an elaborate theoretical device to justify his seeming inconsistency in defending (as he did) Stalin's Terror while Stalin was alive and attacking communism after Stalin was dead and discredited.

There is one conspicuous difference between Sartre's approach to politics and that of Hobbes. Although Hobbes saw violence at the heart of political society, he did not like violence. Hobbes was a sort of pacifist. Better tyranny than war and anarchy for him. But Sartre, like Machiavelli, is partial to a certain amount of well-directed violence. Sartre, like Machiavelli, is discontented with things as they are; more so, he positively detests the bourgeoisie and everything to do with it. So far as socialist regimes are concerned, Sartre seems to echo Hobbes – bad government gives no grounds for rebellion. But where bourgeois societies are concerned, Sartre itches for change; he is impatient for the revolutionary fusion of the series into the socialistic group.

In an interview in January 1962 Sartre said: 'For me, the essential problem is to reject the theory according to which the Left ought not to answer violence with violence.'[1] Note that he says the *essential* problem. Hobbes would never have said this. But Machiavelli might well have done so.

1. *France-Observateur*, 1 Feb. 1962, p. 8.

Camus and Justice

When Albert Camus was killed at the age of forty-six, it was natural to feel, with the shock of the news, that here was a writer cut down in mid-career, his work only half accomplished. But reading his books again, knowing that there is no more to come, one has the quite different impression of an *oeuvre* that is remarkably finished, rounded, complete. In his notebooks[1] Camus himself speaks of death 'giving a form' to life and to love by transforming both 'into destiny', and death, in a way, has given to Camus's own work a form that was not evident before. It was, admittedly, becoming clear enough in his lifetime that Camus was not just an *écrivain engagé* in the sense that was fashionable in the 1950s. His claim was to be an artist. But he was also a moralist in the tradition of Montaigne. Now that we have perforce to see his work as a totality, we can begin to discern what his place in that tradition might be.

There is another short significant entry in Camus's notebook: 'The ethic of the classical French moralists (with the one exception of Corneille) is critical and negative. That of twentieth-century moralists, on the contrary, is positive: it defines *ways of life*.' This is one of the reasons, no doubt, why we are more conscious than were our ancestors that the moralist is a man as well as a writer. Poetry can be isolated from the poet, and history from the historian, but the moralist's voice is personal; his credentials, so to speak, are what he is. The first thing we want to know about a man who 'defines a way of life' is how he lives himself.

Of Albert Camus it must be said at once that his life was, if nothing else, a remarkable triumph over adversity. He looked not

1. *Carnets: janvier 1942-mars 1951*, Paris, Gallimard, 1964, p. 28.

at all like a man who had known hard times, who had been born very poor and been throughout his life repeatedly ill. He had, on the contrary, the proud and easy manner of one accustomed to advantages. Camus not only believed in happiness, venturing to speak a word – *le bonheur* – that had almost fallen from use among French intellectuals of his generation, but he looked happy. In a collection of reminiscences, published in 1964,[1] a compositor who worked on *Paris-soir* when Camus was the editorial secretary during its melancholy months of exile in Clermont-Ferrand in 1940, recalled that whenever Camus came into the printing works '*on a vu d'emblée un rayon de soleil*'.

There is another key word: *le soleil*. For Camus, the sun and happiness went together. 'When I come to look for what is fundamental in myself, I find a taste for happiness,' Camus once told an interviewer. 'At the heart of my work there is an invincible sun.'[2] And in the speech he made when he received the Nobel Prize in 1957, Camus said: 'I have never been able to forget the sunlight, the delight in life, the freedom in which I grew up.'[3] The hardest years of his life had been spent in Algeria, but there, he felt, everything was transmuted by the warmth of nature. In the cold, dark north, he imagined that adversity might be unendurable; in the Mediterranean sun, it was not only bearable, but it could be made, as he himself undoubtedly made it, a school of stoic wisdom.

Camus's parents were working-class French-Algerians, his father a cellarman in the wine trade, his mother, whose family came from Majorca, a domestic servant of humble status. His father was killed on the Marne in October 1914, when Camus was eleven months old. His mother, illiterate and pious, brought up Camus and his elder brother on her earnings as a charwoman. They lived near Algiers in the plebeian suburb of Belcourt, where a family of five – the boys, the mother, the grandmother, and a feeble uncle – was crowded into narrow quarters. But if it was a family that 'lacked almost

1. *Camus* (Collection Génies et Réalités), Hachette, Paris, 1964.

2. *Les Nouvelles Littéraires*, 10 May 1951.

3. Quoted in *Resistance, Rebellion and Death*, trans. Justin O'Brien, London, Hamish Hamilton, 1961, p. 198.

everything', it was also, Camus remembered, one that 'envied almost nothing ... Poverty was never a misfortune for me, for it was flooded with light.'[1] A bursary enabled Camus to go at the age of ten to the *lycée* of Algiers. Scholarship boys in those days were expected to be more industrious than others, and Camus, as a working-class child in a self-consciously middle-class school, early acquired the habits of hard work. He was fortunate in his teachers. As a little boy at the primary school in Belcourt, he was specially coached for the bursary by a teacher named Louis Germain; and when at the age of seventeen Camus entered the *premières lettres supérieures* he became the pupil of an outstanding French-Algerian teacher who was also a writer, Jean Grenier. Camus aspired to become, like Grenier, a philosophy teacher, and went so far in this direction as to write a dissertation on Hellenism and Christianity in the writings of Plotinus and St Augustine. This hope was thwarted. Early in his student career at the University of Algiers, Camus was stricken with pulmonary tuberculosis, a consequence of early malnutrition. The illness was serious, and at one point he was told he was going to die. In the event, he recovered, but he was twice rejected on medical grounds from the *agrégation*, the competitive examination which opens the door to the French teaching profession.

Camus had character enough to make the best of his disappointment. He had already started to work his way through college in the American style, and he continued to earn his living as, among other things, a government clerk, a salesman, a meteorological official, and an actor. It was not until he was twenty-five that he found a more or less permanent niche in journalism. He was to have several recurrences of the disease of his lungs, but his general physique was good. He was an excellent swimmer and an enthusiastic footballer; he kept goal for his university's XI, the Racing Université d'Alger. The team was the one form of collective to which his intensely individualistic nature responded. He sometimes said that football had given him his first lessons in ethics. His upbringing was Christian; but Christianity, which he had seen as his selfish grandmother's substitute for earthly satisfactions, he could never believe to

1. Quoted in *Albert Camus* by Germaine Brée, Columbia University Press, 1964, p. 5.

be true. Nothing could persuade him of the existence of a God of love. At the same time he found that life was intensely worth living. He was, as he afterwards thought of himself, a natural pagan. Indeed, as a youth, he enjoyed life too much to think about it; his response to the world was not one that needed to express itself in words. An uncle of his, a butcher of literary tastes and staunch Voltairean views, tried to interest him in the early writings of André Gide, and lent him a treasured copy of *Les Nourritures terrestres*. But somehow the nephew was not compelled by an author who, however impressive his command of language, nevertheless imparted to his pantheism a faint air of *fin de siècle* corruption; in such lyricism about Mediterranean beauty there was a hint of inauthenticity, a suggestion that the sun and sea and sand were not what the rich northern pederast was really there for. Falseness was something to which Camus was always acutely sensitive. He handed the book back without enthusiasm. Long afterwards he said of this first encounter with Gide, '*Le rendez-vous était manqué.*'[1]

The inspiration that Gide might have given Camus came instead from Jean Grenier, and from a little-known novel which Grenier lent him, *La Douleur* by André de Richaud. This book described a world which Camus recognized as his own; the world of nature and of suffering, of 'a mother, poverty, and blue skies'. As Camus afterwards testified, 'this novel opened up for me the world of creativity'. It gave him the wish to write such a book himself. The actual model for Camus's first book, however, was a collection of essays by Jean Grenier, *Les Iles*, published in 1933, when Camus was twenty. As a stylist Grenier offered perhaps too cerebral and donnish an example for a man of Camus's more spontaneous and instinctive nature. But as a philosopher, Grenier did much to sharpen Camus's awareness of the moral aspects of human experience. The visible world was magnificent, assuredly, and the joy of youth intense; but life was full of injustice and evil. The universe was blind, senseless, and indifferent to human welfare. Grenier thus inspired Camus's belief in what, with the existentialists, he spoke of as *l'absurde*.

Camus's first book, *L'Envers et l'endroit*, was published in Algiers

1. Later, Camus was to appreciate the work of Gide more, and to become one of his friends. See 'Recontres avec André Gide' in *Hommage à André Gide*, 1951.

when the author was twenty-three. He came to be dissatisfied with it as a work of art, and discouraged the reprinting of it, but he could still say many years later, 'For myself, I know that my source is in *L'Envers et l'endroit*, in that world of poverty and light which I inhabited for so long; the memory of it still protects me from two dangers that beset every artist – resentment and self-satisfaction. . . . As for life itself, I know no more than what is said, very clumsily in that book.'

The contrast between the joy of living in the physical world and the metaphysical *absurdité*, or irrationality, of the universe is the common theme of the five essays which make up *L'Envers et l'endroit*. One of these essays deals with a journey Camus made to Prague; and he compares the feeling of estrangement which he has in that cold 'northern' city, where he knows neither the language nor the people, to the feeling of harmony with the external world which he experiences in North Africa. But this feeling of harmony is not one of identification; and Camus draws out a further contrast between the humanized nature of Tuscany (another place he visits) and nature in the altogether more powerful, elemental, savage form which he knows in his own country. Even so, Italy belongs to the south, and the author is happy there; and he insists that the joy of Italy is a sensuous one. What could Italy offer a disembodied spirit? How could a soul live with no eyes to see Vicenza, no hands to touch the grapes, and 'no skin to feel the caress of the night on the road from Monte Berica to the Villa Valmarana'? The book is a form of 'autobiographical travel writing' in which the author tries to explain how the experience of travel has uprooted him, made him shed his unreflective attitudes, and helped him to feel that 'the way to overcome despair is to pit one's own love of life against the indifference of the universe.'

Camus's second book, *Noces*, was published (again in Algiers) in 1938, when the author was twenty-five. It is more assured and accomplished than his first. There is less emphasis on the meta-physical void, and more on the joy of living. The book is full of praises for Algeria and the Algerian people. Camus writes of his walking among the ruins of Tipasa, 'treading the fragrant herbs underfoot, caressing the stones ... opening my eyes and my heart to the unbearable grandeur of a sky radiant with heat'. Later, in the cool shadows he abandons himself 'to the happy lassitude of my union with the world'. Such an abundance of joy in life makes him feel that 'happiness itself is a duty'.

'Light', 'youth', 'the sun', 'the earth', 'the sea'; these are the recurrent images; the style is vivid and compelling, but it is not the kind of writing that lends itself to translation:

Une matinée liquide se leva, éblouissante sur la mer pure. Du ciel, frais comme un oeil, lavé et rélavé par les eaux, réduit par ces lessives successives à sa trame la plus fine et la plus claire, descendait une lumière vibrante qui donnait à chaque maison, à chaque arbre, un dessin sensible, une nouveauté émerveillée. La terre, au matin du monde, a dû surgir dans une lumière semblable.[1]

These books should not be set aside as mere writings of youth. The theme of 'happiness as a duty' is one which never ceased to concern him, and he continued to write essays which celebrate the joy of man's physical contact with the natural world. A selection of essays written between 1939 and 1953 was published in his book *L'Été*, and all bear witness to the continuity of his thought and feeling. He certainly did not 'turn aside', as it is often said, from these preoccupations to politics because of the war. Indeed, at the age of twenty-one (having already contracted a short-lived first marriage), Camus actually joined the Communist Party. He left it twelve months later when, as a result of a direction from Moscow, the party line changed, and ceased for a time to support the claims of the Arabs in Algeria. Camus was also active in these early days in the left-wing *Maison de la Culture* in Algiers. One of his chief interests then was the theatre, and he helped to found two companies with a 'social' orientation, the *Théâtre du Travail*, and afterwards the *Théâtre de l'Equipe*. For the first of these companies Camus wrote, nominally in collaboration with others as a collective enterprise, but in fact with little help, a left-wing political play, *La Révolte dans les Asturies*. This play was banned from the Algerian stage for political reasons, but published in book form in 1935. It also appears in

1. *Noces*, Algiers, Charlot, 1938.

Camus's collected works as the first of the five plays written during his literary career, all of them, except the unsuccessful *Le Malentendu*, political or at any rate 'ethico-political'.

It was his interest in politics which prompted Camus to turn from the theatre to journalism. The opportunity to make his name in this field came in 1938 when Pascal Pia decided to set up in Algiers a radical newspaper to compete with the powerful and reactionary *Écho d'Alger*. This was the *Alger-républicain*, and Pia offered Camus a job as reporter and editorial writer. The work was not well paid, but it enabled Camus to write what he wanted to write. He did a certain amount of literary and dramatic criticism, but his most important contributions were on social problems in Algeria. Camus's articles drew attention to the poverty of the Arabs, to the disadvantages under which they laboured as second-class citizens, and he reported in detail on various cases of injustice and inequity. His *Enquête en Kabylie* was a memorable and thoroughly documented study of maladministration. But while everything he wrote was critical of the French government, he was never anti-French; he did not trade in the clichés of nationalism and revolution; he did not look for any sweeping or total answer to Algeria's complex problems. His appeal was always reasonable; his articles were addressed to particular abuses which needed a remedy and specific evils which cried out for reform. This attitude to politics was, once he had left the Communist Party, characteristic of Camus all his life.

Among the book reviews which Camus wrote for the *Alger-républicain* was one, published in October 1938, of Sartre's first novel, *La Nausée*. This review gives a good inkling both of what was later to unite, and of what was later to divide these two writers. Where Sartre's novel depicted the universe as irrational, meaningless, purposeless and godless, Camus felt it touched the truth. The rejection of the Cartesian Christian cosmology was wholly in accord with Camus's own attitude. But where Sartre's hero, Roquentin, not only asserts this metaphysical *absurdité*, but reacts with disgust and sickness against the physical world, Camus is at variance with Sartre. The physical world nauseates Roquentin because it is 'viscous', 'slimy', 'oozing', 'soft'. He hates the daylight and the sun and the heat. Roquentin tells himself: 'I shall do nothing good except perhaps after nightfall – because of the sun.' He yearns for the relief of darkness; and when it comes, he says: 'I am content – the cold is so pure, the night is so pure.' *Purity* – that is what Roquentin cares about; and Camus recognized in Sartre the true voice of the northern puritan, of the metaphysician *manqué*, something directly opposed to the Mediterranean sensibility which he himself was trying to articulate.

One of Camus's more paradoxical works is his *Mythe de Sisyphe*, an existentialist essay written *contre les existentialistes*. Camus wrote *Le Mythe de Sisyphe* between 1938 and 1941. It is a book with a sensational beginning. 'There is only one truly serious philosophical problem', Camus writes, 'suicide'. This puts the reader in mind of Proudhon's opening salvoes: it makes one sit up. Camus explains that he is not going to develop an argument demonstrating the irrationality of the universe; he takes that *absurdité* as a starting-point. His problem is not metaphysical, but moral. His problem is: if the universe has no meaning, how can a man's life have any meaning? And if a life has no meaning, why should a man not end it? This is what makes suicide the only *problème philosophique vraiment sérieux*.

The answer that Camus suggests is that each man can give life a meaning by giving his own life a meaning. There is no justification for suicide, either in the physical or the philosophical form. 'Philosophical suicide' is Camus's striking way of describing the response of such existentialists as Kierkegaard who react to the irrationality of the universe by a 'leap into faith'. The man who commits physical suicide destroys his own body; the man who retreats to religion does the same violence to his own mind or reason. Even so the difficulty remains, just how is one to give one's own life a meaning? The lesson of *Le Mythe de Sisyphe* is that one should live intensely, drinking the cup of experience to the full, *vivre le plus*. Moreover, one must do this knowing that life, as such, has no ultimate purpose. The limited purpose it has is man-given not God-given. So we must never expect too much. This is where Sisyphus fits into the picture; he keeps pushing the same stone up the same hill, but he knows what he is doing, and finds what joy there is to be found in it. The last words of Camus's essay are almost as memorable as the first: 'We must imagine Sisyphus happy.'

Thus the view of life which Camus develops on the basis of *l'absurde* is one that revives the thought of various moralists of the ancient – and, as we ought perhaps to add, of the Mediterranean – world: stoicism, Epicureanism, Cyrenaicism, all of which taught in their different ways that 'happiness is a duty'. But plainly happiness is not the only moral value which is honoured in *Le Mythe de Sisyphe*. There is also, for example, *lucidity* (the need to see clearly, especially oneself and one's predicament) and a virtue which goes with lucidity, *authenticity* or sincerity, the need to be true to one's affirmations, to act as one believes. (For what else is moral belief?) On these two last principles, Camus's views were strikingly in harmony with those of Sartre. Hence when Camus developed the themes of lucidity and authenticity in a book he wrote at about the same time as *Le Mythe de Sisyphe*, namely, his first novel, *L'Étranger* (*The Outsider*), it is not surprising that that novel should have been received, as it was, by Sartre with acclamation.

Meursault, the hero of *L'Étranger*, is not a man who has learned to '*vivre le plus*'; he is bored, passive, slack; in the heat of the Algerian sun, he drifts rather than acts, and fate seems to dominate his life. He is seen by the author as a very *ordinary* man; Camus once explained in a newspaper interview: 'The men in Algeria live like my hero, in an absolutely simple manner. Naturally you can understand Meursault, but an Algerian can understand him more easily and deeply.' Meursault, however, has one supreme virtue, honesty. He does not pretend to feel what he does not feel, or to believe what he does not believe. His honesty is his undoing. On the day the story begins, Meursault learns that his mother has died. He feels no great grief, and shows none; he smokes and sleeps through the vigil, and the day after the funeral he meets a girl and goes to a comic film. Later Meursault gets involved in a brush with some Arabs; an Arab pulls out a knife, 'the sunlight flashed on the steel'; Meursault happens, by chance, to have a revolver, and the trigger 'gives way under his fingers'. When Meursault is charged, he says

5

calmly that he killed the man 'because of the sun', and in the course of the trial, witnesses are called to say how callously he had behaved at his mother's funeral. Meursault is regarded by the shocked bourgeois judges as an obvious 'born criminal' and he is condemned to the guillotine. Then in the death cell, Meursault comes to life; when the chaplain offers him salvation in the world to come, Meursault answers, with passion, that this world is the only place where happiness can be known. In prison, he tells the chaplain, he has learned to find joy in the intensity of experience. Even if his cell had been as small as a tree-trunk, Meursault says he would have found a reason for living, looking through an opening and waiting for the birds to pass, or watching the changing shapes of the clouds in the sky.

Between 1936 and 1938, Camus had written the first draft of a novel which he entitled *La Mort heureuse*. Dissatisfied with this work, he discarded it unfurnished, and it was not published until eleven years after his death in the first of a projected series of 'Cahiers Albert Camus'.[1] It was rumoured before its publication to be an early version of *L'Étranger*; it turns out to be the story of a man who seeks happiness, even at the cost of crime, and the name of its hero 'Mersault' closely resembles 'Meursault' of *L'Étranger*. But it is a mistake to regard *La Mort heureuse* as an early draft of the later novel. In the first place, it is a failure, and one can readily understand why Camus dropped it. In fact, it is hardly a novel at all, but an attempt to give some of the material of his early Cyrenaicist essays a fictional form. *La Mort heureuse* is a shapeless, diffuse work with no unifying vision, where *L'Étranger* is a supremely well structured and concentrated example of the philosophical novel.

There is, however, one book which does throw some light on the origins of *L'Étranger*, and that is a novel by Claude Aveline, *Le Prisonnier*, which was first published in 1936. Camus was acquainted both with Aveline and his work. At a time when the two writers were supporters of the Popular Front, Aveline, a left-wing liberal, visited Algeria to give some lectures on Anatole France, whose

1. *Cahirs Albert Camus, I: La Mort heureuse.* Ed. Jean Sarocchi, Paris, Gallimard, 1971.

protégé he had once been, at the Maison de la Culture in Algiers.[1] Camus received Aveline at the Maison de la Culture, and broadcast about him on Radio Algiers praising *Le Prisonnier*.[2] Between this novel of Aveline's and Camus's *L'Étranger* there is a curious identity of opposites. *Le Prisonnier* is a brilliant short novel, in the French classical tradition, about a man reflecting on the murder he is about to commit. The murder is a deliberated crime, prompted by the intelligible desire to avenge a gross humiliation. The author takes a logical, if ironical, view of the human passions, and the whole book is influenced by a kind of liberal rationalism which (despite Aveline's Russian origins) is very French and cartesian. *L'Étranger* is an equally short novel, no less well-structured, the style elegant and spare; the subject again the killing by one man of another and the thoughts and memories of a man in prison. But the perspective of *L'Étranger* is the antithesis of *Le Prisonnier*. Human experience is seen to be without rational coherence; motives are ambiguous: even the 'crime', if it is a crime, on which the whole narrative turns, is obscure: was it culpable homicide, an accident, an act of self-defence? We do not know. Meursault is punished by the world he lives in because he will not play the game according to its rules. He strives only for authenticity; the living reality of experience does not fit into the logical categories of the French republican tradition. Whether *L'Étranger* is to be reckoned an existentialist novel or not, Meursault is undoubtedly an existentialist hero.

L'Étranger was an immediate success when it was first published in Occupied France in 1942. It was Camus's first book to be published in Paris, and it gave him his national reputation. Sartre, already well known, was one of the book's most forceful and effective champions.[3] And like Sartre's own writing, *L'Étranger* seemed to speak directly to the mood which was prevalent in France in those years of defeat. Both writers were concerned to go into and through and beyond despair to some positive affirmation; to negate the negation.

1. *Jeune Méditerranée*, Algiers, April 1937, carries a report of the occasion, with contributions by Camus and Aveline.
2. On 19 Feb. 1937. 'Présentation de Claude Aveline par Albert Camus'.
3. See Sartre's review in *Cahiers du Sud*, February 1943.

In an entry in his notebook Camus explains that 'the subject of *L'Étranger* is mistrust of formal virtue'. He adds: 'Everything I have ever thought or written has to do with this mistrust.' But he speaks of the danger to which this attitude is subject: 'People who have felt this mistrust in themselves have gone on to suspect *any* declared virtue, and then it is only a step to suspecting *genuine* virtue.'

Long before *L'Étranger* and *Le Mythe de Sisyphe* were published Camus had come to feel that 'genuine virtue' entailed something more than lucidity and authenticity and 'living to the full'. It required a positive effort and even sacrifice to diminish the amount of injustice and oppression and violence in the world. This line of thinking, which had prompted his political activity, was one about which, in 1942 and 1943, when *L'Étranger* and *Le Mythe de Sisyphe* were published, Camus was compelled to keep silent. But by that time he was already a member of the Resistance.

Shortly before the war began, his newspaper, the *Alger-républicain*, had been changed into the evening *Soir-républicain*, and Camus appointed an editor. The army rejected him on medical grounds (he had had to go to the Savoy Alps for more treatment in 1938), but his life as an editor was made intolerable by the military censors. Finally, the Governor-General of Algeria was so incensed by Camus's uncooperative attitude that he suppressed the *Soir-républicain* by a decree dated 10 January 1940, and 'advised' Camus to leave Algiers. Camus found a job in Paris on the *Paris-soir*, but rather than write for a controlled press, he took on the purely administrative duties of 'editorial secretary'. After a few months with this paper, first in Paris then in Unoccupied France, Camus returned to North Africa – not to Algiers, where he was still *persona non grata*, but to Oran (his second wife, Francine, was an *Oranaise*). He worked there as a teacher for a time in a private school patronized by the Jewish community. In the summer another haemoptysis forced him to go once more to France for treatment, which he received at Le Chambon-sur-Lignon. When he was well enough, he joined a Resistance movement operating in the region of Lyons and St Étienne. Camus was always extremely reticent and modest about his career in the Resistance, but he is known to have taken part in several hazardous operations, including the production of the clandestine newspaper *Combat*. He was once arrested by the Gestapo with proofs of *Combat* in his possession, but contrived to bluff his way out of the situation. In 1943 he was sent as representative of his Resistance group to Paris, where he also found a job (which he kept for the rest of his life) as a reader with the publisher Gallimard.

The line of thought which carried Camus into the Resistance may be discerned in a play he wrote as early as 1938, although it was not performed until the end of the war: *Caligula*. The theme of this play was suggested to Camus by the famous remark of Dostoevsky that 'if God does not exist, everything is permitted'. Camus felt passionately that this was not true: God does not exist; and everything is *not* permitted. His *Caligula* is based on the record of Suetonius; he is a man who believes that 'everything is permitted': an emperor who rules cruelly, capriciously, destructively. He is not an unreflective man; he follows his destructive policy even though he sees it will bring about his own destruction in the end. He has a certain 'lucidity' and 'authenticity'. But Caligula is not the hero of the play. The voice of the author is heard in those who oppose him, especially in Cherea. And their point of view is simple: there is no way of *proving* by rational argument that Caligula is wrong; he cannot be *refuted*. Nevertheless, he must be *resisted*.

The idea of 'resistance' figured in Camus' own thinking well before events in France made the word fashionable. It was to remain a central concept in all his work. During the war, he wrote and first published clandestinely in 1943, a series of letters to a German friend who had become a Nazi. Camus explains in the fourth of these *Lettres à un ami allemand*, that he began from the same 'philosophical starting-point' as his correspondent – a recognition of *l'absurde*. But whereas the German friend had gone on from this to nihilism, and from nihilism to a blind commitment to the irrational creed of Hitlerism, he, Camus, had found himself thrown back on 'a fierce love of justice, which, when all was said and done, seemed to me as irrational as the most sudden passion'. Camus continues:

Where lay the difference? Simply that you readily accepted despair and I never yielded to it. Simply that you saw the injustice of our condition to the point of being willing to add to it, whereas it seemed to me that man must exalt justice in order to protest against eternal injustice, create happiness in order to protest against the universe of unhappiness. Because you turned your despair into intoxication, because you freed yourself from it by making a principle of it, you were willing to destroy man's works and to fight him in order to add to his basic misery. . . .

I, on the contrary, chose justice in order to remain faithful to the world. I continue to believe that this world has no ultimate meaning. But I know that something in it has a meaning and that is man, because he is the only creature to insist on having one. This world has at least the truth of man, and our task is to provide its justification against fate itself. And it has no justification but man; hence he must be saved if we want to save the idea we have of life.[1]

This excerpt, together with his early play *Caligula* and the articles he wrote for the *Alger-républicain*, should be evidence enough to refute the commonly held view that Camus was originally a naïve Cyrenaicist, a mere champion of *vivre le plus*, until the experience of the Occupation 'converted' him to political commitment; he was never 'converted' – and this is one thing which distinguished him from such intellectuals as Sartre and Gide, who have the temperament of converts; Camus' attitude to moral and political questions was remarkably steady and consistent throughout his life. It was always a main endeavour of Camus to avoid extremes. When he spoke about 'Mediterranean wisdom' he meant something directly opposed to what he called 'northern Germanic ideologies'. In his notebooks he wrote:

The whole effort of German thought has been to substitute for the notion of human nature that of the human situation, and thus to put history in place of God and modern tragedy in place of classical equilibrium. Contemporary existentialism pushes this effort even further and introduces into the idea of situation the same uncertainty as in that of nature. Nothing remains but movement. But like the Greeks, I believe in nature.[2]

1. *Resistance, Rebellion and Death*; trans. Justin O'Brien, London, Hamish Hamilton, 1964, p. 21.
2. *Carnets*, 1942–51, p. 174.

In another entry he wrote: 'For the Greeks beauty is at the start. For a European it is an end scarcely ever reached. I am not modern.'

Moderation as a primary political virtue is the subject of Camus's most controversial book, *L'Homme révolté* (*The Rebel*). This was not published until 1951, but some of the ideas it contains were sketched in a little-known essay, 'Remarque sur la révolte', that Camus wrote in the war years for a collection edited by Jean Grenier.[1] This begins with a much-needed explanation of what Camus meant by *l'homme révolté*. It is a curious thing about Camus, that despite his being one of the best prose stylists of his generation, he had a certain partiality for words which suggest something different from what he meant to say, and often, something more extreme. '*L'absurde*' is one such word; '*la révolte*' is another. '*La révolte*' is usually translated into English as 'rebellion', and '*L'homme révolté*' as 'the rebel', both terms commonly connected with the ideology of violent change. But this is precisely what Camus is *not* upholding. He writes at the beginning of his 'Remarque sur la révolte': 'What is an *homme révolté*? In the first place he is a man who says *no*. But in refusing, he does not renounce. He is also a man who says *yes*.'

Camus goes on to give the example of a civil servant who complies with orders up to a certain point, and then refuses to obey. This refusal, says Camus, is not negative; for it affirms the man's belief in something which is sacred, inviolate; it reveals a point beyond which he will not go. The man who says *no* manifests his conviction that certain things are wrong and his own refusal to do them; indeed his refusal to do them is inseparable from his belief that they are wrong. Camus is concerned with the question, 'Can man alone, and without divine aid, create his own moral values?' The *homme révolté* is the man who answers 'yes' to this question with his deeds as well as his words. So part, at least, of what Camus means by the *homme révolte* is simply 'a man of principle', a man who bears witness to the reality of his moral values by his conduct.

On 21 August 1944, the day of the liberation of Paris, *Combat* appeared for the first time as an openly published newspaper in the

1. *L'Existence*, ed. Jean Grenier, Gallimard, 1945.

capital; and Camus, already the outstanding contributor to its clandestine numbers, became the editor. These were the days of national unity, and Camus found himself not only a well-known intellectual, but a fashionable leader of opinion. In the months which followed the liberation, his editorials in *Combat* were buoyed up with left-wing enthusiasm, filled with calls for friendship for the Soviet Union, attacks on the industrial cartels in France, and pleas for a 'working-class democracy'. These editorials also called for stern measures against former collaborators, but Camus became increasingly disturbed at the growth of anti-fascist intolerance as a reaction to fascist intolerance. 'One result of the war and Resistance,' he said in an interview in 1957, 'was the temptation of hatred. To see your beloved friends and relations killed is not a good schooling in magnanimity. But this temptation to hatred had to be overcome.'

The years that followed the liberation were not easy for Camus. 'They were marked', he afterwards said, 'by the experience of a solitary struggle.' He had friends, assuredly, but they went different ways from his. One such friend was Sartre. They met for the first time in 1944, and found they had much in common, but also many differences. As early as November 1945, Camus said in an interview: 'Sartre and I are always astonished to see our names connected. We are even thinking of publishing an advertisement declaring that we have nothing in common and each refusing to honour the debts the other contracts!' However, it was the things which united them which seemed most important in the early years of the peace. Sartre himself was then passing through what might be called his 'Kantian' phase, holding the views expressed in *L'Existentialisme est un humanisme* where he argued that as men must 'will freedom for freedom's sake,' they 'must will freedom for all,' and that in legislating for oneself in moral conduct one is legislating for all humanity. However, Sartre soon repudiated the argument of this lecture as 'a mistake', and moved rapidly towards his later creed of 'existentialized Marxism'. Indeed for a time in Simone de Beauvoir's words, Sartre 'chose the U.S.S.R.', and having chosen the U.S.S.R. he became one of the most bitter critics of Camus, who continued to believe, as he always believed, in saying *no* to injustice, including the injustice of Stalin.

It was in these early postwar years that Camus wrote what is perhaps his most 'political' novel, *La Peste* (*The Plague*). Here the theme is not merely resistance to injustice, but the setting of good against evil. *La Peste* is both a novel and an allegory, although Camus writes of it in his notebooks as 'a pamphlet'.[1] Camus's plague is set in Oran. After a fairly leisurely description of the city, the action begins with a characteristically arresting opening: 'On the morning of April the sixteenth, Dr Bernard Rieux stepped out of his front door and stumbled on a dead rat in the middle of the landing.' When he comes home that evening the doctor sees a rat dying with blood streaming out of its mouth. To the reader these rats are, of course, the heralds of the plague. But Dr Rieux does not think at once of this: 'The burst of blood from the rat's mouth threw him back on his own anxious thoughts. His wife, who had been ill for a year, was to leave next morning for a sanatorium in the mountains.'

The novel owes some of its success to the way in which the author relates public to private disasters. In one sense, the plague is an allegory of war; like the defeat of France in 1940, the plague brings at the same time public corruption and private grief, bereavements, separation, suffering. Dr Rieux is a man who transcends his private grief by devotion to public duty. It is not that he is conventionally patriotic, still less has he any religious faith. His devotion is to a certain image he has of man. He is a humanitarian of what we might call the 'Camusian' kind. He is confronted in the story by a humanitarian of another sort, more extreme, more *exalté*, more Tolstoyan – a 'lay saint' named Tarrou.

Tarrou represents a point of view for which Camus had a great respect, belief in total non-violence, of turning the other cheek and answering evil only with good. Tarrou, in the novel, comes to Oran to be close to that human suffering which he has made it his business in life to relieve. Organizing 'sanitary squads' to help combat the plague, he meets and makes friends with Dr Rieux. One evening Tarrou tells the doctor his life story. He is the son of a public prosecutor, originally destined for the law himself. One day when he was seventeen he attended a murder trial, and gazing at the shrunken figure of the prisoner, for whom his father was demanding a death

1. '*La Peste* est un pamphlet': Camus, *Carnets*, 1942–51, p. 175.

5*

sentence, young Tarrou had suddenly revolted against the practice of answering murder with murder, and against the kind of society which relied on the death penalty. Thus Tarrou had become an agitator against the bourgeoisie, an extremist of the Left. Then having seen a deviationist shot by a communist firing squad, he came to realize that he was upholding the very evil he was supposed to be fighting. So Tarrou had abandoned the militant left and become a champion of 'constructive pacifism'; he will now support no one who uses violence, and what strength he has he will use to relieve suffering.

Although this is a point of view which Camus respected, it was not one he could share. There is a notable conversation in the book between Tarrou and Dr Rieux, in which the doctor's voice is discernibly that of Camus:

'In the end,' said Tarrou with simplicity, 'what interests me is to know how one could become a saint.'

'But,' said Rieux, 'you don't believe in God.'

'Precisely. Could one be a saint, without God? That is the only concrete problem that matters to me today.'

'Perhaps,' said the doctor. 'But you know I myself feel more solidarity with people who are defeated by life, than I do with saints. I have no taste, I suppose, for heroism or for holiness. What interests me is being a man.'

'Well, yes,' said Tarrou. 'We are looking for the same thing. Only I am less ambitious.'

Rieux thought that Tarrou was speaking lightly, and he looked up at him. In the dim light of the evening, he saw a face that was both serious and melancholy.[1]

Elsewhere in the novel there is a conversation between Dr Rieux and Father Paneloux, an exponent of the Christian, or at any rate the Angustinian view that the plague is an evil sent by God to punish sinners. Paneloux tries to persuade Dr Rieux that they are both working for man's salvation. 'Salvation is too big a word for me,' the doctor says, 'I don't aim so high. What I am concerned with is a man's health.' On another occasion he says: 'The best way to struggle against the plague is by being honest.' And once more, talking about his work for victims of the plague, Dr Rieux protests:

1. *La Peste*, ed., W. J. Strachan, London, Methuen, 1959, p. xxxi.

'There is no question of heroism in all this, it's just a matter of common decency.'

This emphasis on 'common decency' is important. As Professor Philip Thody has shrewdly said, Camus 'had the feelings of the common man and the mind of an intellectual'.[1] But while Camus believed in a kind of virtue which was ordinary, in every man's reach – in honesty, fairness, magnanimity, tolerance, and the doing of one's duty – he did not imagine this was an easy thing to believe in. It is Tarrou, who believes in sainthood, who says to Rieux: 'I am less ambitious.'

In 1947, when the newspaper *Combat* was being subjected to various political and commercial pressures, Camus withdrew from its staff. But he did not, in any sense, withdraw from politics. He made several appeals on behalf of political prisoners – including Communist prisoners in Greece and Nationalist prisoners in Tunisia; he supported Garry Davis's campaign for world citizenship; he wrote, with Arthur Koestler, a forceful pamphlet against the death penalty, *Réflexions sur la guillotine*. He attracted particular attention when he denounced the Stalinist terror in Russia, but he was equally unequivocal in his denunciation of Franco's régime in Spain. When Franco's Spain was admitted to UNESCO, Camus resigned from its committees; his play *L'État de siège* was set in Spain, and was clearly directed against dictatorship in that country. In an open letter to Gabriel Marcel who had criticized him for attacking Spain in this play, Camus wrote: 'No one in good faith can fail to see that my play defends the individual, the flesh in its noblest aspects – in short, human love – against the abstractions and terrors of the totalitarian state, whether Russian, German, or Spanish.'

If his attitude to Spain offended the Right, it was his denunciation of tyranny in Russia which alienated the Left. But this estrangement was not merely a difference of attitude to the Soviet Union. It was a moral difference. When the fellow-travellers held that 'dirty hands' were inevitable in politics, Camus denied that the end justified the means. This led to a direct collision with Sartre. For Sartre, as he put it, was trying to teach the Left to 'answer violence

1. *Albert Camus*, 1913–1960, Hamish Hamilton, 1961.

with violence,' while Camus held that the only violence that was permissible in politics was 'the force that is needed to suppress violence'.

The full extent of Camus's estrangement from the Left became apparent in 1951, when he published *L'Homme révolté*. This is a systematic statement of his case against political violence, or what Camus calls *crimes de logique*. Just as in *Le Mythe de Sisyphe*, he argued that there was no valid way to justify suicide, so in *L'Homme révolté*, he holds that there is no sound philosophical argument to justify 'the necessary murder', crimes, such as acts of revolutionary violence, which are committed on principle. The teaching of *L'Homme révolté* is that one should beware of ideological extremism, and seek to improve the condition of man's life on earth by measured, practical, and gradual reform. The book is a plea for moderation, or *la mesure*.

To the charge that such a method is ineffective in politics, Camus replies that on the contrary 'it is the *only* method that is efficacious today.' There are, he suggests, 'two sorts of efficaciousness: that of the typhoon and that of the dew.' In politics only the latter is really efficacious. Extremism is merely efficient: it can seize and even keep power; but it destroys creative life.

To kill freedom in order to establish the reign of justice comes to the same as resuscitating the idea of grace without divine intercession and of restoring by a mystifying reaction the mystical body in its basest elements. Even when justice is not realised, freedom preserves the power to protest and guarantees human communication. Justice in a silent world, justice enslaved and mute, destroys mutual complicity and finally can no longer be justice. The revolution of the twentieth century has arbitrarily separated, for over-ambitious ends of conquest, two inseparable ideas. Absolute freedom mocks at justice. Absolute justice denies freedom. To be fruitful, the two ideas must find their limit in one another.[1]

Again, Camus argues that absolute non-violence is impossible just as absolute freedom is impossible: force is needed to combat violence; but the *homme révolté* will take up arms 'only for institutions which limit violence, not for those which codify it'. As for the

1. *The Rebel*, trans. Anthony Bower, New York, Vintage Books, 1956, p. 291.

plea that the 'end justifies the means', Camus replies that it is means which will justify the end. To sacrifice oneself is to confer a certain dignity on the end but to sacrifice others for a noble ideal was to rob that ideal of its nobility.

It was already clear from his brief sketch of 1944, *Remarque sur la révolte*, that Camus did not mean by an '*homme révolté*' what we should ordinarily call a rebel: here he makes it even clearer that his theory of *la révolte* is directly opposed to one of revolution. Camus places the revolutionary ideologies of the modern world in the tradition of nineteenth-century nihilism. They seek to annihilate the real in order to actualize the ideal. This he sees as totally opposed to a genuine theory of *la révolte*, which would seek to modify, to correct, to reform the real. Manifestly one cannot reform what one annihilates. Revolution, as Camus sees it, is thus essentially destructive, while *la révolte* preserves in order to improve. This is the basis of the charge that Camus's theory is 'conservative'; in the sense that Camus insists that you cannot change if you annihilate, the word is perhaps permissible; but the central point is a call for change, for change in the name of freedom and justice. He also writes in favour of forms of democratic trade union socialism which accept the necessity of toleration and *la mesure*.

In *Les Temps Modernes* in May 1952, there appeared a bitter attack on *L'Homme révolté* by Francis Jeanson, the most militantly Left of Sartre's disciples. Jeanson accused Camus of a quietism which played into the hands of the *bourgeoisie*, and thus being 'objectively' reactionary. In opposing revolutionary violence, Camus was, according to Jeanson, like the Hegelian 'beautiful soul' which wished to be uncontaminated by physical reality. As for Camus's reference to the typhoon and the dew, Jeanson asked what was the good of the dew *against* a typhoon – or the violence of capitalism? 'To our incorrigibly bourgeois eyes', Jeanson wrote, 'it is very possible that capitalism has a less "terrifying" face than Stalinism, but what kind of face does it present to a miner or a state employee victimized for striking, or to a Madagascan tortured by the (French) police, to a Vietnamese "cleaned up" by napalm, or a Tunisian "nabbed" by the Foreign Legion?'

This attack prompted Camus to write, at Sartre's invitation, an open letter to the Editor of *Les Temps Modernes*, but in the same number Jeanson returned to the attack on Camus for his 'anti-communism', arguing that while it was impossible to speak simply of Stalinism, Stalinism must nevertheless be respected because it commanded the support of the French working-class and because it represented a necessary stage on the way to authentic revolution. Sartre gave Jeanson his complete support, and in a magisterial letter to Camus, Sartre declared: 'Our friendship was not easy, but I shall regret it. It you break it now, then no doubt it had to be broken. A lot of things united us; a few divided us. But those few were already too many' (*Les Temps Modernes*, August 1952).

In the course of *L'Homme révolté*, Camus makes repeated claims for his theory of *la mesure* being *méditerranéenne*, he talks a great deal about *la pensée solaire* and of the south being opposed to the dark Germanic ideologies of the north:

The history of the First International, when German socialism cease-lessly fought against the libertarian thought of the French, the Spanish and the Italian, is the struggle of German ideology against the Mediterranean mind. The masses against the State, concrete society against absolutist society, measured freedom against rational tyranny, finally altruistic individualism against the colonisation of the masses, are thus contradictions which express, once again, the endless opposition of moderation to excess which has animated the history of the occident since the time of the ancient world.[1]

In thus claiming moderation to the 'southern', Camus has been reproached, with some reason, for failing to appreciate the strong element of moderation in the Anglo-Saxon democratic tradition, which is undoubtedly 'northern'. This is perhaps the more odd in view of Camus's great interest in English and American literature, and his particular debts to Defoe and Melville.[2] The truth may be that the Anglo-Saxon democratic tradition is, from Camus's point of view, too pragmatic and anti-philosophical, and also too closely

1. Ibid.

2. It is also worth mentioning that the two best books about Camus's work are by English critics, Philip Thody's *Albert Camus 1913–1960*, Hamish Hamilton, 1961; and John Cruickshank's *Albert Camus and the Literature of Revolt*, Oxford University Press, 1959.

linked with Puritanism. The liberalism of Camus, if liberalism it is to be called,[1] is essentially anti-puritan. For Camus, however much he may have reason to emphasize his belief in the principles of justice, liberty, duty, and *la mesure*, never ceased to believe also in the more pagan ideal of 'living to the full'. The last novel he published is a piercingly ironical study of a certain puritan type which Camus detested and dreaded, the 'judge-penitent'.

La Chute is, like *L'Étranger*, a short narrative told in the first person. Its central character has the biblical sounding name of Jean-Baptiste Clamence (the language and idioms of religion are used with great effect throughout the book). Clamence is self-exiled in the dark, damp northern city of Amsterdam, where he sits in a café on the Zeedijk, waiting for anyone who will listen to his confessions and confess in turn to him. He is, as he explains, a judge-penitent; he judges himself when he has confessed and he will judge others when they confess. His story is that he was once a lawyer in Paris, living well, enjoying success with women and so forth, until one day he heard a girl's cry coming from the Seine; he did nothing to help her, and since then he has been tormented by guilt. This knowledge of his own guilt enables him to understand others. He is an expert on the guilty conscience. He relishes in turn the sensation of his own sinful nature and that of 'a charming repentance'.

By a number of subtle strokes, Camus brings out the intolerable narcissism and bogusness of Clamence; in his bedroom he has a stolen picture by Van Eyck, 'The Just Judges', and he dreams of the day when a detective will arrest him and put him in prison. He wants his punishment, just as he wants others to be punished. Or does he? The novel ends with the words: 'Now it is too late. It will always be too late. Fortunately.' Camus was thinking a great deal at the time he wrote this book about the type of guilt-ridden bourgeois

1. There are points of resemblance between Camus's political thought and that of Sir Karl Popper who belongs to the Kantian liberal tradition, not to that of Anglo-Saxon empirical social-democracy. There are many interesting parallels to be discerned between *L'Homme Révolté* and both *The Open Society* and *The Poverty of Historicism* of Popper. Philip Thody tells me that Camus possessed a copy of *The Open Society*.

intellectual which was very prominent in St Germain-des-Prés, the kind of man whose guilt comes out in a generalized hatred for existing society, and who, wanting punishment for himself, would bring punishment on the whole nation. It would be fanciful to see in Jean-Baptiste Clamence any lineaments of Jean-Paul Sartre, but Camus's anti-hero is, in many ways, the typical Sartrian hero. Germaine Brée has spotted an interesting parallel between Clamence and Sartre's Saint Genet. She writes:

In 1952 Sartre had published his extensive psycho-analysis of Jean Genet, *Saint Genet, Actor and Martyr*. 'Actor and Martyr' – the words fit Jean-Baptiste Clamence perfectly. A thief and jail-bird, and a writer to boot, Genet, Sartre suggested, is a kind of scapegoat, virtually thrown out of the city walls with the secret evils of society magically heaped upon him, a thoroughly Sartrean interpretation. He became thereby in Sartre's eye 'one of the heroes of our time', in fact an image and symbol of what we are fated to be, denizens of an impotent society, incapable of 'the leap' that would put us on the right side of history. Clamence's hollow voice seems curiously to echo Sartre's, as Camus leaves him, in his rhetorically built 'cell of little ease', on the brink of a leap he will never take, free to accumulate a sterile guilt with which he inoculates others.[1]

There is a significant use of the expression 'judge-penitent' in an essay Camus wrote (with Sartre in mind) in April 1958, on the Algerian question:

If some Frenchmen consider that, as a result of its colonising, France (and France alone among so many holy and pure nations) is in a state of sin historically, they do not have to point to the French in Algeria as scapegoats ('Go ahead and die; that's what we deserve!'); they must offer up themselves in expiation. As far as I am concerned, it seems to me revolting to beat one's *mea culpa*, as our judge-penitents do, on someone else's breast.[2]

La Chute has been variously interpreted, and perhaps more often misinterpreted, for irony is a dangerous device. Jean Bloch-Michel has revealed an earlier version of *La Chute* in which Clamence, like

1. Germaine Brée, *op. cit.*, pp. 41–2.
2. 'Preface to Algerian Reports', quoted in *Resistance, Rebellion and Death*, p. 87.

Meursault in *L'Étranger*, awaken in the last few pages to a new kind of articulateness; but in the final Clamence remains – as we feel he should – a prisoner of his own rhetoric.

The political situation in Algeria, which had been of minimal interest to metropolitan Frenchmen (including the Left) in the 1930s, when Camus was working for the *Alger-républicain*, became in the 1950s a question which overshadowed all others. Feelings became intense and extreme. Nationalist sentiment was captured by the left-wing F.L.N.; and the reaction was an equally violent movement for *Algérie française*. Camus continued to plead for moderation. He did not want to see the left-wing Arab nationalists impose their will by terrorism in Algeria or the French administration upheld by counter-terrorism. He hoped for reconciliation between all the races in Algeria, and for a programme of reconstruction in association with the French economy. In a broadcast on Radio Algiers in 1956 he made an eloquent appeal for a 'truce' in what had already become a bloody civil war.

When this plea was ignored, Camus made no more political speeches on the Algerian question. He was in many ways a disappointed man. To most of the French Left, who had not only come out on the side of the F.L.N., but were even advocating desertion from the French Army in Algeria (and, in certain cases, actively helping the Arab terrorists), the name of Albert Camus became anathema, particularly when he refused to sign various protests which were got up against the French Army's atrocities in Algeria, because the authors of these protests refused at the same time to condemn the F.L.N. atrocities. Camus wrote: 'When violence answers violence in a growing frenzy that makes the simple language of reason impossible, the role of intellectuals cannot be, as we read every day, to excuse from a distance one of the violences and condemn the other.' He added: 'It seemed to me both indecent and harmful to protest against tortures in the company of those who readily accepted Melouza or the mutilation of European children; just as it seemed to me harmful and indecent to condemn terrorism in the company of those who are not bothered by torture.'

The antipathy of the 'committed' French Left intellectuals did not perhaps, by this time, greatly wound Camus; but he was dismayed by the hardening of people's feelings in Algeria, where both Arabs and French were dehumanized by the competing ideologies of nationalism and imperialism. Some of this sorrow can be detected in the last book of fiction he published before his death, *L'Exile et le royaume*. Because it is a group of stories, and not a novel, this book has never had the attention which has been given to Camus's larger works, though it may prove to be one of the most enduring. The prose style is of the highest order. The self-consciousness of the earliest work is gone, and the intricacy of the writing in *La Chute* is abandoned in favour of a simpler and more direct idiom. There is one story in *L'Exile et le royaume* which might be read as an allegory of the author's own relationship with his native country. It is called 'L'Hôte' and the hero is a French Algerian schoolmaster in a mountain village.

One day the local gendarme brings an Arab prisoner to the schoolmaster, orders him to take charge of the man, and escort him the next morning to the nearest prison. Although the prisoner is a murderer – not a political assassin – the schoolmaster cannot bear the thought of being a jailer. So next day he takes the Arab towards the nearest cross-roads. He points the way towards the prison and the way towards a nomad's encampment, where the man could shelter from the police. He gives the Arab food and leaves him. Later he looks over his shoulder to see how the man is faring, and observes him walking, not towards the nomads, but towards the prison. And this is not the final irony. When the schoolmaster gets back to school, he sees that some Arabs have chalked on his blackboard: 'You have handed over our brother. You will pay for this.'

Experience had done much to instruct Camus in the irony of life. Indeed, if he had had any religious sentiments, they would probably have been those of Thomas Hardy, believing in a Providence that sheltered the wicked and punished the innocent. There was even an irony in the circumstances of Camus's death. On 4 January 1960, having bought himself a railway ticket for Paris, he accepted a lift from his publisher, Michel Gallimard; for no apparent reason, the car swerved off the road and hit a tree; they were both killed.

Michel Foucault:
A Structuralist View
of Reason and Madness

In France Michel Foucault once enjoyed, or at any rate experienced, a fashionable success akin to that of the *nouveau roman*. For a philosopher – and Foucault is a professional philosopher, with a chair at the Collège de France – such fame is unusual. There is nothing in the titles of Foucault's books to suggest a wide appeal: *Maladie mentale et personnalité*,[1] *Folie et déraison*,[2] *Naissance de la clinique*,[3] *Raymond Roussel*,[4] *Les Mots et les choses*[5] and *L'Archéologie du savoir*[6] – three books about sickness and madness, one about a pre-surrealist (or aleatory) writer who killed himself, and two books about language. Henri Bergson himself, one imagines, could not have commanded the attention of *le tout Paris* if he had discoursed on such subjects; even Sartre had to make his name as a novelist before he was noticed as a philosopher. Yet here is Foucault, with his high seriousness and melancholy themes, an instantaneous hit.

His impact was perhaps not entirely unwilled. He came before the public very much as a *nouvelle vague* or 'with it' figure, a spokesman of his generation. In an interview with Madeleine Chapsal, Foucault said: 'One realized very suddenly about fifteen years ago that one was very very far removed from the preceding generation, that of

1. Paris, Presses Universitaires de France, 1954.
2. Plon, 1961; trans. by Richard Howard as *Madness and Civilization: a history of insanity in the age of reason*, New York, Random House, 1965; London, Tavistock Publications, 1967.
3. Paris, Presses Universitaires de France, 1963.
4. Paris, Gallimard, 1963.
5. Paris, Gallimard, 1966.
6. Paris, Gallimard, 1970.

Sartre and Merleau-Ponty and *Les Temps Modernes.*' Asked who this 'one' was, he answered:

The generation of people who were less than twenty years old during the war. We recognised Sartre's generation as undoubtedly courageous and generous, with a passion for life and politics and existence – but we, we have discovered another thing, another passion, a passion for concepts and what I shall call 'system' (*La Quinzaine littéraire*, 16 May 1966).

He is a brilliant writer, in the manner of Maurice Blanchot, rhetorical, paradoxical, dialectical; but whereas Blanchot's style is rebarbative and rather German, Foucault's is mellifluous, repetitious and fast. His originality is more questionable. Foucault himself speaks of drawing on sources that the French do not know about because the French with their 'monoglot narcissism' ignore foreign scholarship. He mentions Cambridge historiography, Anglo-American logical theory, the 'new' criticism, German philosophy (he was at the *Institut Français* in Hamburg), and he declares himself a follower of Nietzsche. He also acknowledges his obvious debt to Blanchot.[1] Yet, running through all his work are curious echoes and reverberations, not of neglected theorists, but of those very much received today by the younger intellectuals of France, of Louis Althusser, a Marxist, who was once Foucault's teacher, of Jacques Lacan, Marcel Mauss, Roussel, Dumézil, and above all of Claude Lévi-Strauss. It is perhaps this very mixture of the familiar and unfamiliar, of the *chic* and the esoteric, which holds one clue to the popular success of Foucault's work; that, and (as one cannot help feeling) a certain sensational quality it has. Foucault names the Marquis de Sade as his favourite writer next to Nietzsche: the preference is revealing. Foucault's work has a significant place in the fashionable cult of violence. Dr David Cooper, the British existentialist psychiatrist, who would perhaps prefer to be called an 'anti-psychiatrist', writes, in a preface to the English version of Foucault's *Folie et déraison* (*Madness and Civilisation*): 'The true significance of (this) book resides most precisely in the terror that it may produce in a significant few of us.'

1. Foucault is a member of the editorial board of three which runs the Paris literary periodical *Critique*, in the pages of which the influence of Maurice Blanchot is often very marked.

But even apart from such morbid thrills, Foucault's writings are most enjoyable, in spite of their titles. His *Folie et déraison*, which is also known by its alternative or subtitle, *Histoire de la folie à l'âge classique*, begins with an account of the decline of leprosy in modern Europe, and the closing of the lazar-houses, followed in sequence by the opening of places of confinement for the mad. A 'history' the book is called, but it is far from Foucault's intention to give us an account of madness on the lines that a history of leprosy might be written, tracing its spread and development and changes down the ages. On the contrary, Foucault holds that madness is not a disease at all.

Madness, he claims, is a form of knowledge which the dominant culture of the seventeenth and eighteenth centuries could not understand. Madness, he goes on to say, is fusion of reason and unreason; and he denies that reason has any objective privilege over unreason. In the Age of Reason there ceases to be any 'dialogue' between the 'sane' and the 'insane' because unreason does not speak and reason no longer speaks to unreason.

In the serene world of mental illness, modern man no longer communicates with the madman: on the one hand, the man of reason delegates the physician to madness, thereby authorising a relation only through the abstract universality of disease; on the other, the man of madness communicates with society only by the intermediary of an equally abstract reason which is order, physical and moral constraint, the anonymous pressure of the group, the requirements of conformity. As for a common language, there is no such thing; or rather there is no such thing any longer; the constitution of madness as a mental illness, at the end of the eighteenth century, affords the evidence of a broken dialogue, posits the separation as already effected, and thrusts into oblivion all those stammered, imperfect words without fixed syntax, in which the exchange between madness and reason was made. The language of psychiatry, which is a monologue of reason *about* madness, could only be established on the basis of such a silence.[1]

This 'silence' is what Foucault sets out to explore. He claims that it is something characteristic of the modern world. In the Middle Ages and until the Renaissance, man's dispute with madness was a

1. *Folie et déraison*, Paris, Plon, 1961, p. 9.

'dramatic debate in which he confronted the secret powers of the world'. The medieval understanding of madness was coloured by images of the Fall and the Will of God, of the Beast and the Metamorphosis, and of all the marvellous secrets of Knowledge. Moreover, the Middle Ages gave madness a relatively minor place in the hierarchy of vices. As the opposite of prudence, it was one of the twelve dualities which disputed the sovereignty of the human soul. At the Renaissance, madness leaves that modest place and moves to the forefront. It also becomes exceedingly disturbing. Foucault quotes from various Renaissance authors who assign to madness the privilege of reigning over whatever is bad in men. In Shakespeare and Cervantes, again, madness occupies, he suggests, 'an extreme place', in that it is shown to be beyond appeal; nothing ever restores it either to truth or to reason; it leads only to laceration and thence to death.

'But very soon', Foucault continues, 'madness leaves these ultimate regions where Cervantes and Shakespeare had situated it, and in the literature of the early seventeenth century it occupies, by preference, a median place ... madness is no longer considered in its tragic reality, in the absolute laceration that gives it access to the other world; but only in the irony of its illusions.'

Thus there emerges that understanding of madness which is characteristic of the seventeenth and eighteenth centuries, '*l'âge classique*' or 'the Age of Reason'.

The great threat that dawned on the horizon of the fifteenth century subsides, the disturbing powers that inhabit Hieronymus Bosch's painting of the Ship of Fools have lost their violence. Forms remain, now transparent and docile, forming a cortège, the inevitable procession of reason. Madness has ceased to be – at the limits of the world, of men and death – an eschatological figure; the darkness has dispersed on which the eyes of madness were fixed and out of which the forms of the impossible were born. Oblivion falls upon the world navigated by the freed slaves of the Ship of Fools. Madness will no longer proceed from a point within the world to a point beyond, on its strange voyage; it will never again be that fugitive and absolute limit. Behold it moored now, made fast among things and men. Retained and maintained. No longer a ship but a hospital.[1]

1. Ibid., p. 50.

The curious thing was that in spite of having tamed the violence of the voices of Renaissance madness, the Age of Reason did not wish to hear them at all. The 'hospital' that Foucault speaks of was essentially a place of confinement. Foucault detects an analogy between the medieval attitude to lepers and the Age of Reason's attitude to madmen. When the Middle Ages banished lepers from society, such men were thought of as having been delivered up to God. To abandon a leper was not, to the medieval mind, an açt of disservice; to exclude him from the company of ordinary people, to shut him up in lazar-houses, was to speed him on the way to salvation. When leprosy disappeared from Europe, the same formula of exclusion remained – but it fastened on to a new object, and the men who were thenceforth to be redeemed by confinement included, notably, the mad.

It is common knowledge that the seventeenth century created great houses of confinement, especially in France. Foucault claims (but does not document the claim) that as many as one out of every hundred inhabitants of Paris were locked up, madmen together with criminals, pederasts and vagabonds. The most famous 'hospital' was the Hôpital Général, an institution which had nothing to do with medicine, but a great deal to do with the absolutist politics of the Bourbon kings: soon after its foundation in 1656 there were as many as 6,000 people within its walls. The Hôpital Général was primarily intended to suppress begging: a 'modern' solution to an ancient problem. Later it was modernized still more effectively when work was given to the unfortunates who were put inside, and people who had once been a drain on charity were made to contribute to the prosperity of all.

Foucault offers three forms or layers of explanation for this phenomenon. The first is more or less sociological; that is, he suggests that the attitude of the Age of Reason towards madness was governed by dread. 'Until the seventeenth century,' he writes, 'evil in all its most violent and inhuman forms could not be punished unless it was brought into the open.' But the Age of Reason preferred to hide things away, fearing that some aspects of evil had such a power of contagion and contamination that publicity must necessarily multiply them. Only oblivion could suppress them. The 'hospital' was a place where the evil of madness could be concealed, isolated, and forgotten.

But Foucault is not satisfied with this explanation, and passes to a more philosophical or existentialist one: 'Ultimately,' he writes, 'confinement did not seek to suppress madness . . . the essence of confinement was not the exorcism of a danger. Confinement merely disclosed what madness, in its essence, was; a manifestation of non-being; and by providing this manifestation, confinement thereby suppressed it, since it restored it to its truth as nothingness. Confinement is the practice which corresponds most exactly to madness experienced as unreason, that is, as the empty negativity of reason; by confinement, madness is acknowledged to be *nothing*.'

Besides this sociological and this metaphysical explanation, Foucault also adumbrates, if he does not fully state, an economic one: the mad are bundled together with vagabonds and criminals because they are all members of the same economic class, now felt to be a burden and embarrassment to the rising capitalist order. In an article about Foucault in *Critique* (May 1965), François Dagonet sums up the argument of this section of the *Folie et déraison* with these words: 'On the one hand, the empty lazar-houses invited, awaited new guests. And the bourgeois did not fail to install in the Hôpital Général eccentrics, delinquents, nymphomaniacs, homosexuals, blasphemers, infidels, the idle – all those who compromised the good ordering of social space.' The expression 'bourgeois order', with its Marxist implications, is Dagonet's, not Foucault's: but it is a perfectly valid reading of what Foucault is saying. Indeed it is arguable that the Marxist notion of 'infrastructure' plays a crucial role in his theory.

However this may be, Foucault passes from considering the attitude to madness which belonged to the Age of Reason to consider that which belonged to the nineteenth century. For this, on his view, was another distinct epoch. It was the age of psychology, the age in which the different forms of insanity and mental disturbance were assigned 'scientific' names. Foucault argues that the chief significance of these innovations was to give madness a new content of guilt, of moral sanction and just punishment which was no part of the experience of the Age of Reason. Nineteenth-century psychiatry reduced madness to the status of a mere disease. 'Madness', as Foucault puts it, 'was now detached from its truth, which was unreason', and was henceforth 'nothing but a phenomenon adrift and insignificant upon the undefined surface of nature'.

Foucault's appraisal of nineteenth-century medicine as a method of introjecting guilt into disease may remind some readers of Dr Alex Comfort's book, *The Anxiety Makers*;[1] Foucault's view of asylums as places of punishment has clear affinities with the argument of Dr R. D. Laing and his 'Dialectics of Revolution' group, who regard conventional psychiatry as being itself a form of violence, a method of beating a nonconforming individual into submission to established social norms. And Foucault himself returns to the attack in a further work, *Naissance de la clinique* (1963), in which he moves from the field of madness to that of sickness in general, and describes the nineteenth-century hospital, the so-called place of healing, as yet another place of confinement. But the main object of criticism in this short but richly polemical essay is the positivist assumptions on which the claims of nineteenth-century medicine to be a science rested. Anatomy and pathology – the cutting up of dead bodies as a means of discovering the secrets of the living – inspire some of Foucault's most vigorous scorn:

> The sovereignty of the visible. And even more imperious than that, the power of death. That which hides, and spreads the curtain of night over Truth is, paradoxically, life. Death, on the contrary, opens to the light of day the dark box of the human body: life is dark, death is clear: the oldest conceptual values of the western world meet in here in a strange inversion, which is the very direction of pathological anatomy. . . . The medicine of the nineteenth century was haunted by that occult eye which cadaverises life.

The nineteenth century, the age of positivism, is clearly the period that Foucault most dislikes. But at the end of it comes Nietzsche – and also Freud, to whom Foucault pays a fervent tribute:

> Between Freud's *Five Case Histories* and Janet's scrupulous investigations of *Psychological Healing*, there is more than the density of a *discovery*; there is the sovereign violence of a *return*. Janet enumerated the

1. London, Nelson, 1967.

elements of a division, drew up his inventory, annexed here and there, perhaps conquered. Freud went back to madness at the level of its *language*, reconstituted one of the essential elements of an experience reduced to silence by positivism; he did not make a major addition to the list of psychological treatments for madness; he restored, in medical thought, the possibility of a dialogue with unreason. Let us not be surprised that the most 'psychological' of medications has so quickly encountered its converse and its organic confirmations. It is not psychology that is involved in psycho-analysis, but precisely an experience of unreason that it has been psychology's meaning, in the modern world, to mask.

Some guide to an understanding of Foucault's writings on madness may be found in his later writings on language, especially *Les Mots et les choses*, which is perhaps his most ambitious work to date. The continuity between the two is insisted upon by the author. In the preface to the later book he explains that whereas *Folie et déraison* was a history of the *other*, *Les Mots et les choses* is a history of the *same*. This somewhat obscure remark was itself explained by Foucault in an interview:[1]

Folie et déraison was, broadly speaking, the history of separation, the history above all of a certain division which every society finds itself obliged to institute. In *Les Mots et les choses*, on the other hand, I wanted to write the history of order, that is of the way in which a society reflects the resemblances of things among themselves and the way in which the differences between things can be mastered, organised in networks, arranged according to rational schemes. *Folie et déraison* is the history of difference; *Les Mots et les choses* the history of resemblance, of the same, of identity.

As in the earlier book, Foucault depicts the past as being divided into very distinct periods. Indeed it is the main argument of *Les Mots et les choses* that there are two great splits or discontinuities to be observed in the *episteme* of western culture: the first, which inaugurates the Age of Reason in the first half of the seventeenth century, and the second at the beginning of the nineteenth century, which marks the threshold of modernity.

The key to the *episteme* or the *savoir* which is central to a culture,

1. With Raymond Bellour, in *Les Lettres françaises*, 21 March 1966.

is, Foucault says, language. In Europe before the Age of Reason, he suggests, language existed in its simple and primitive condition. Language in the sixteenth century was part of the world: things were then understood as both revealing and hiding their enigma as language. Words were regarded as a special sort of thing: things to decipher. Between words and things there was thus a kind of unity: and the link between the sign and what was signified was *resemblance*. Foucault adds:

> Up to the end of the sixteenth century resemblance helped to construct the knowledge that belonged to western culture. It was resemblance which, to a large extent, shaped the exegesis and the interpretation of texts, resemblance which organised the use of symbols, which permitted acquaintance with visible and invisible things, and guided the art of representing them. The world revolved around itself; the earth repeated the sky; faces were reflected in the stars; and plants contained within their stems secrets for the service of man. Painting imitated space. Representation, whether in art or in learning, took the form of repetition: being a theatre of life or a mirror of the world, such was what gave all language its validity, its mode of proclaiming itself and of formulating its right to speak.[1]

Foucault distinguishes four types of similitude. First, there is *convenientia*, or the resemblance of proximity and harmony, such as that of the body and the soul, or 'the great chain of being'. It is a similitude which pertains less to individual things than to the whole in which they find themselves: the world is the home of a universal *convenientia*. Secondly, Foucault distinguishes *aemulatio*. Here the similitude is between things not proximate, but separated by space, as in the example of a face and its image in a glass: the 'great chain of being' is here no longer joined, though its divided links still confront each other across a gap; there is such a similitude between Man and God, between the light of the eyes and the light of the sun. Thirdly, there is *analogy*, a familiar notion in both Greek and medieval philosophy, where the resemblance is not visible but only conceivable. And fourthly, there is the type of resemblance which rests, as Foucault puts it, on the play of *sympathy* and *antipathy*. 'Sympathy', he writes, 'is an instance of the *Same* so powerful and so

1. *Les mots et les choses*, Paris, Gallimard, 1966, p. 32.

imperious that it is not content to be one of the forms of similitude; it has a dangerous power of assimilation, of rendering things identical with one another, of uniting them, of making them disappear as individual entities.' So sympathy has to be compensated by its twin, antipathy, which preserves things in their separateness and prevents assimilation: 'The identity of things, the fact that things can resemble and approach each other without fusing together but while still preserving their individuality, is the result of constant balancing of sympathy and of antipathy which replies to it.'

Foucault goes on to suggest that the ruinous weakness of this type of *episteme*, and of the concept of similitude on which it rested, is that it was imprisoned within itself: the sixteenth century mind was 'condemned to knowing only the same thing.' Knowledge was confined to things that are capable of resembling each other. And it is because of this conceptual defect, according to Foucault, that the *episteme* of the sixteenth century gave way to another, and (as he believes) radically different one, that of the Age of Reason. The philosophers of the Age of Reason were all against the theory of similitudes: Bacon the empiricist no less than Descartes the rationalist. In that new age representation was to take the place of resemblance.

Foucault sees Cervantes's Don Quixote as a key figure at this crucial moment of European thought. All the travels and adventures of Cervantes's hero can be seen, he suggests, as a 'quest for similitudes': and the important thing is that Don Quixote is disappointed.

Don Quixote negates the world of the Renaissance; the written word ceases to be the prose of the real world; resemblances and signs are no longer united; similitudes are deceptive, they lead to visions and frenzies; things cling obstinately to their ironical identity; things are no longer anything but what they are; words wander at random, without content, without resemblances to give them substance; they no longer denominate things, but sleep between the leaves of dusty books.

Signs, which were once regarded as keys to knowledge, are understood in the Age of Reason as being coexistensive with representations. As signs, all representations became part of an immense ordered network. For the Age of Reason does not merely introduce new thoughts, it reconstitutes the whole system of thought. And the limit of knowledge becomes the perfect transparency of representations in the signs which order them.

The significance of Descartes for Foucault is not that Descartes was the founder of 'rationalism', but that he introduced analysis in place of analogy as the method of enlarging knowledge. 'Henceforth all resemblance would be submitted to the test of comparison; that is to say, it was not accepted unless it was certified by measurement, by common unity, or, more radically, by the order, the identity and the series of differences.' Cartesian truth was to be formed in clear and distinct ideas. The Leibnizian project of establishing a mathematics of qualitative order was central to the thought of the Age of Reason. Not that its thinkers concentrated on mathematics as such: but rather that the whole *episteme* or *savoir* of the age was based on a mathematical concept of order. Hence its characteristic *taxinomia*: the arrangement of all identities and differences in categories. 'General grammars' are devised to guarantee the complete intelligibility of words; 'natural histories' are constructed to classify things and animals in rigid lines; theories of exchange are invented to explain the circulation of wealth. Language itself becomes the analysis of thought, not in the simple sense of a 'cutting up', but analysis understood as 'the profound inauguration of order in space'. This, in turn, leads to the union of speech and understanding – to know is to speak correctly. Vocabulary becomes a 'bible of knowledge'. To speak, to clarify, to know – all these are strictly 'of *the same order*'. The basic task of discourse is to assign a name to a thing, and with this name to name its being.

Thus, Foucault continues, for two centuries of modern culture, discourse took the place of ontology. When it named the being of representation in general it was philosophy – the theory of knowledge and analysis of ideas; when it assigned to each represented thing the name which fitted it, it was science – nomenclature and *taxinomia*. This is Foucault's explanation of the coherence which exists throughout the Age of Reason between the theory of representation and the theories of language, of natural history and of wealth.

At the beginning of the nineteenth century this configuration changed entirely. The theory of representation was discredited: and thus could no longer serve as a general basis for all possible order; and the notion of language as a spontaneous picture of things and as the necessary medium between representations and beings, vanished in its turn. Natural history gave way to biology: theories of wealth to political economy.

What had happened? The modern mind had become conscious of the limits of representation: and representation as an *idée clef* was jettisoned even as similitude had been two centuries earlier.

At the beginning of the 19th century, words recovered their old, their enigmatic density. But this was not to restore them to the map of the world they had inhabited at the Renaissance, nor to bundle them together with things in a reciprocal system of signs. Detached from representation, language existed thereafter – and has continued to exist until our own time – only as a scattered mode; for philologists, words are like so many objects thrown up and left behind by history; for those who seek to formalise, language has shed its concrete content, and reveals only abstract forms of discourse.[1]

Once again the figure of Nietzsche appears towards the end of the story as an angel of intellectual deliverance. For at the end of the nineteenth century, language makes its 'return to the field of thought', because Nietzsche then makes 'a radical reflection on language' the task of philosophy.[2] Language is restored, reborn. And Foucault's love of paradox finds satisfaction in a further irony: the rebirth of language, under Nietzsche's auspices, coincides with the death not only of God, but of Man. 'Man', Foucault is able to say on the last page of *Les Mots et les choses*, 'is an invention of recent date; and perhaps of an imminent end'.

One of the problems in appraising Michel Foucault's books is to decide what *kind* of books they are. So far I have spoken of them as 'histories', and this is a word that Foucault himself often uses.

1. Ibid., p. 315.
2. Foucault thus makes for Nietzsche a claim which is often made for Wittgenstein; see, for example, Justus Hartnack's *Wittgenstein and Modern Philosophy* (Methuen, London and Doubleday, New York, 1965).

Indeed in certain respects, they might seem to belong to that field of inquiry which has become very lively in recent years, intellectual history or the 'history of ideas'. But Foucault does not much care for this category. Books on the history of ideas, he protests (justly with regard to many of them), are chronological accounts of theories, philosophies, movements of opinion: whereas he himself is not interested in theories or *Weltanschauungen*. What interests him, he says, is the logic of the concepts out of which the *episteme* of an epoch is constructed.

As a name for this enterprise, he prefers not 'history' but 'archaeology'. He explained his use of this term in his interview with Raymond Bellour:

> By 'archaeology' I wish to name not a discipline exactly, but a field of research, which could be described as follows: In any society, the knowledge, the philosophical ideas, the ordinary day-to-day beliefs, and, moreover, the institutions, the commercial and political practices, the social customs – all these lead us back to a certain implicit *episteme* which belongs to that society. This *episteme* is profoundly different from the knowledge found in the scientific books, the philosophical theories, the religious apologetics, but it is what makes possible the appearance, at a given moment, of theories, beliefs, practices.

Foucault seeks this *episteme* in the widest possible study of the literature, the documents, the institutions, the whole 'archive', as he calls it, of the period. His 'archaeology' is, in his own words, 'the science of that archive'.

I do not myself feel that this novel employment of the word 'archaeology' is to be welcomed. 'Archaeology' has already a generally understood use in English as 'the systematic study of the remote past'; and the word *archéologie* in French has the same meaning: '*Étude des civilisations anciennes grâce aux monuments figurés et aux objets qu'il en restent*', as it is expressed in the *Grand Larousse Encyclopédique*, vol. i (1960).

To stipulate a new definition for a word which has already a fairly unequivocal meaning in ordinary use is to spread confusion, and not light.[1] This is perhaps a greater fault in Foucault since he seems to

1. See on this subject R. Robinson, *Definition*, Oxford University Press, 1950, p. 80.

believe that the ambiguity of words can prove highly destructive. At any rate, he suggests in his study of the pre-surrealist poet, *Raymond Roussel*, that there was a direct connection between Roussel's passion for exploring and exploiting the different and conflicting meanings which the same word can bear and Roussel's ultimate suicide.[1]

To treat Foucault as a historian may, in view of his claim to be something else, be unfair. However, it must be said that as a writer of what is, at least, about the past, he has a marked and oddly old-fashioned weakness: that of detecting radical 'splits' or *coupures* in man's past experience which do not, on a closer scrutiny, appear to be at all clear-cut, if they are there at all. The past can, of course, be said to fall into periods which sometimes (but rarely) correspond to the arbitrary division of time into centuries. But the strict periodization is more an invention of textbooks than a feature of history itself.

Nor are Foucault's boldest statements about the past backed up with any evidence. His method is too often that of argument by assertion. For example, Foucault writes: 'No life in the Age of Reason, and no science of life, and no philology either. But "natural

1. This is perhaps to oversimplify Foucault's analysis of Roussel. But see Rayner Heppenstall's essay on *Roussel* (Calder and Boyars, 1966), where he speaks of the 'abysses' in 'any picture of reality revealed by the fact that similar words may signify dissimilar things, that indeed identical words may signify things between which there is no element of identity whatever'. Heppenstall continues:

'According to M. Foucault, Roussel's adventuring among those abysses led inevitably to his suicide. That Roussel's death took place on the actual threshold of a locked door has too much dazzled M. Foucault with its metaphorical and symbolic possibilities. M. Foucault is too fond of labyrinths, keys and thresholds, too anxious to find in Roussel's moment of death a culmination of the pattern of his work, seen too exclusively in terms of the tendency first to mystify, then to explain.... Nevertheless I do not find M. Foucault's argument wholly foolish. The human world is very largely made up of words and their resonances. Most ways of life are framed within a few accepted *clichés*, and to discover that they are meaningless is as quick a road to despair as any. Roussel's lifelong preoccupation with words that may be taken in two or more senses, or which, sounding alike, point in opposed directions, can hardly have failed to suggest to him that all words are treacherous and so that there *are* abysses in any picture of reality.'

history" and "general grammars". Equally no political economy. Instead there existed in the seventeenth and eighteenth centuries a notion . . . or rather a domain: this domain, the field and object of "economy" in the Age of Reason, is that of *wealth*.' None of this is supported by the work of specialists in the subjects Foucault names. William Letwin, in his *Origins of Scientific Economics*,[1] shows that political economy was not a new thing in the nineteenth, or even in the eighteenth century; the studies of Daniel Mornet, Réné Hubert, Ernst Cassirer, and others, place the 'general grammars' of the Enlightenment within a long tradition; and the continuity between what was actually done under the name of 'natural history' in the eighteenth century and what was actually done under the name of 'natural science' in later generations is attested by all the recognized histories of science, which are, of course, different from histories of the theories of science. The 'splits' or *coupures* take place in the realm of the 'isms', the realm of ideologies and speculation, and even there the element of novelty or innovation is limited: for example, Destutt de Tracy, the first of the *Idéologues*, saw himself only as the successor of Condillac and as his propagandist in a more democratic age.

Foucault rests much of his argument on the claim that 'representation' played a central role in the *episteme* of the Age of Reason; and no one can deny its importance. And yet this whole notion of representation was vigorously attacked during this same period, at different levels, by several eighteenth-century theorists – Rousseau, for example, and Burke and Blake. And what about Kant?

Now Kant has rather a special significance with regard to Foucault's enterprise. For it is instructive to compare what Foucault is attempting with what Kant was doing when he inaugurated what he called his 'Copernican revolution'. Kant conceived of himself as having reversed the long-standing assumption of European philosophy that our knowledge to be true must correspond to the properties of the external world; and to have put forward instead the view that the external world must conform to our knowledge. We can make no statement about what the universe really is, Kant claimed; all we can say is that if it is to be an object of understanding, it must satisfy certain conditions that the mind lays down. The

1. London, Methuen, 1963.

mind imposes its own categories and concepts on the universe so as to make sense of experience. *The Critique of Pure Reason* could almost be regarded as an explanation of the conditions of sanity: if we did not have our notions of substance, cause, space, time, to make the world intelligible, we should be mad.

Foucault might well be thought to have taken this exceedingly general and abstract argument of Kant's and then to have given it a local and diminished reformulation: whereas Kant speaks of the human mind in terms of the permanent problem of knowledge, Foucault speaks of 'the mind of Europe' in terms of its changing patterns of belief. In his earlier writings on madness, Foucault dwells on the manner in which the mind of Europe in the Age of Reason prized its sanity, and in doing so he puts that sanity into question. In his later writings on language, he moves on to further challenge. Here it is not so much a case of knowledge imposing its own concepts on the world to make the world intelligible but of different 'periods' conceiving the world in different ways.

The truth of the matter, I believe, is that Foucault is doing something wholly different from Kant. What he is writing is not philosophy, any more than it is history or archaeology; it is a type of 'philosophical anthropology' very like the work of Claude Lévi-Strauss. Foucault's 'structuralism' is structuralism *à la* Lévi-Strauss; that is to say, it is an attempt to understand cultures, or societies, by unveiling the structures of conceptual thought which inform their understanding of the world and their behaviour.[1]

1. In an interview, published in *La Quinzaine littéraire* (1–15 March 1968), Foucault objected to the use of the name 'structuralist' in a manner which implied that people with quite different interests constituted a coherent group. This was part of Foucault's 'reply to Sartre'; but not the better part. Sartre had said, among other things, that the structuralists were a kind of last bastion of the bourgeoisie against Marx; and Foucault, in his reply, recalled that when he, fifteen years before, had been for a few weeks a member of the French Communist Party, Sartre himself was described in the Party as the 'last bastion of bourgeois imperialism.' Foucault added: 'I note with amused astonishment that same phrase coming from Sartre's own pen.'

A fair rejoinder. Nevertheless Sartre was surely justified in regarding the structuralists as having enough in common to be grouped together. The 'category mistake' which does figure in recent French controversies is the one entailed by comparing Structuralism and Existentialism as if they were 'isms' of

Lévi-Strauss's method is too complex to admit of a brisk epitome, but its importance for Foucault can be seen in one or two of its central features. Lévi-Strauss argues that the objective world, the raw natural environment in which man finds himself, is deeply bewildering, but that man, being a thinking creature, is also a constructing creature, albeit a rather amateurish one, like a handyman or jack-of-all-trades in his untidy shed, and he makes order out of the chaos that surrounds him with the aid of any tool that comes to hand. Members of any given society, having a certain shared experience, and enjoying relationships of exchange, including language, construct their own world in a distinctive way. The world man knows is thus not an empirical entity, containing things which he passively perceives; it is a collective representation, governed by man's natural and logical demand, as a thinking being, for some kind of order. This is why Lévi-Strauss, even in his role as an anthropologist, is primarily concerned with the structure of thought itself. He tries in his work to show how each society or culture has a particular system of categories or cognitive scheme which determines the way the people born into that culture apprehend the universe. But while Lévi-Strauss denies that such a system of categories can be deduced from the first principles (which is what he seems to regard as Kant's position), and insists that we have to study various actual societies (and thus be anthropologists) to see how different peoples conceptualize their environment, he also maintains that the degree of variety as between one conceptual scheme and another is limited; and just as Roman Jakobson, the structural philologist with whom he once collaborated, argues that

---

the same sort. Sartre's existentialism, as Foucault himself rightly says, is a totalizing philosophy, a comprehensive metaphysical system in the grand tradition of Hegel, whereas the concern of structuralism, or rather of those who are called structuralists, is 'much less ambitious, much more limited, much more localised'.

It would be interesting to quote at length from the same interview, but unfortunately Foucault himself repudiated the published version, protesting in a letter to the Editors of *La Quinzaine littéraire* (15–31 March 1968) that the text had appeared without his consent and that 'cuts, rearrangements and re-editing have produced a meaning which is foreign to mine. . . .'

all languages are constructed out of a limited number of linguistic essentials or universal characteristics, Lévi-Strauss argues that all cognitive systems must have certain common features. The demand for order is universal; it is a feature of thinking mind as such; every group will construct its own system, but all those systems will bear a distinct family relationship.

These considerations led Lévi-Strauss in *La Pensée sauvage* (1962) to stress the high level of abstract reasoning underlying the cognitive systems of even the most primitive tribes. And if the name 'structuralist' is anything more than a mere label or ticket, it must surely, in Lévi-Strauss's case, relate to the primary importance he gives to the construction, at the highest level of thought, of such conceptual schemes.

Foucault can, I think, be best understood as attempting to explain the cultural history of Europe in the light of this theory which he has in common with Lévi-Strauss. He takes Europe as being a temporal sequence, so to speak, of different cultures (admittedly having some essential features in common, as all cultures have); and then, in asking what is the *episteme* of this or that 'period', Foucault is asking, as Lévi-Strauss might ask, what is the conceptual scheme by which that 'period' gives order and coherence to experience. Unfortunately, Foucault's adaptation of this structuralist method is open to more than one objection. The first, as we have seen, is that the so-called 'periods' of European history, the Renaissance, the Age of Reason, the nineteenth century and the rest, do *not* constitute distinctive entities, analogous to the tribes and cultures which anthropologists examine. Secondly, Foucault offers nothing which corresponds to an anthropologist's study in depth of a given society; instead of 'field work', he singles out richly impressionistic highlights, such as a Cervantes novel, or a Velasquez painting, or the Hôpital Général, which are at best significant clues or keys.

The second characteristic of Foucault's method, which is equally a characteristic of Lévi-Strauss's, is his attachment to the binary principle. This is something as old as Heraclitus and Proclus, though it is undoubtedly thanks to Hegel that it is so much the vogue in France today. It embodies the belief that life is composed of opposites in tension which men attempt to resolve symbolically when they cannot resolve them actually. The binary principle is also a central notion of Jakobson's type of structural linguistics; the notion that opposites – true and false, good and evil, positive and negative – must constitute the framework of any system of logical order. In applying this 'dialectical' way of thinking to anthropology, Lévi-Strauss detects a tendency of any structure, considered historically (or, as he might prefer to say, diachronically), to produce an inverted image of itself. The young rebel against the old, fashions turn upside down, successive generations repudiate, as well as perpetuate, what they inherit.

This binary principle is something which Foucault employs with great gusto and brilliance in depicting the relationship between the different 'periods' he analyses. Having first chopped them up, and proclaimed so to speak, their independence one of another, he then puts them together 'dialectically' with the aid of the binary principle. The Renaissance is rendered intelligible as an inversion of the Middle Ages; the Age of Reason is seen as a mirror image of the Renaissance, and so forth.

The trouble with Foucault here is not that the technique itself is unacceptable. Employed on a modest scale to deal with a certain range of problems, as it is used by Jakobson at any rate, it can be exceedingly enlightening. But the binary principle does not lend itself to the service to which Foucault seeks to put it. Something employed to explain everything, ends up by explaining nothing.

The Pessimism of
Herbert Marcuse

In the year 1955 Professor Herbert Marcuse published a book of radiant optimism. It bore the modest title *Eros and Civilisation: a philosophical enquiry into Freud*,[1] but what it contained was a spirited rejoinder to Freud's belief that civilization depends on repression. Marcuse argued that a non-repressive civilization is a possibility. We had only to remove the repressive elements which belong to political domination, he suggested, and men could live peaceably together in freedom. Moreover, once the unnecessary repressive forces were eliminated, human instincts would be transformed and lose their destructive features. Indeed, Marcuse not only used the word 'would', he sometimes used the word 'will', notably towards the end of his book. For instance, having predicted that the Freudian death-wish would vanish in a non-repressive culture, Marcuse wrote: 'Death would cease to be an instinctual goal. It remains a fact, perhaps, even an ultimate necessity – but a necessity against which the unrepressed energy of mankind *will* protest, against which it *will* wage its greatest struggle [my italics].'[2]

The optimism of this treatise is not marginal, for the central purpose of its argument was to reverse Freud's pessimism. What Marcuse set out to do was to refute the implication of Freudian theory 'that the humanitarian ideals of socialism are humanly unattainable'. He resisted the use of the word 'utopian' as a word of condemnation, whether by psychoanalysts or anyone else: 'Theology and philosophy today compete with each other in celebrating death

1. *Eros and Civilisation: a philosophical enquiry into Freud* (Beacon Press and Vintage Books, 1955).
2. *Eros and Civilisation*, p. 215.

as an existential category; perverting a biological fact into an ontological essence, they bestow transcendental blessing on the guilt of mankind which they help to perpetuate – they betray the promise of utopia.'[1]

Marcuse himself in *Eros and Civilisation* upheld the promise of utopia. Only he did not sustain his buoyant optimism. In his next book, *One-Dimensional Man*,[2] his mood was lugubrious and his conclusion despairing. This book is a study of, or more exactly an attack on modern and especially American industrial civilization. On the last page Marcuse wrote:

> The critical theory of society possesses no concepts which could bridge the gap between the present and its future; holding no promise and show- ing no success, it remains negative. Thus it wants to remain loyal to those who, without hope, have given and give their life to the Great Refusal . . . *Nur um der Hoffnungslosen willen ist uns die Hoffnung gegeben* [It is only for the sake of those without hope that hope is given to us].[3]

In an essay written at about this same time for a book on Babeuf,[4] Marcuse employed the word 'utopian' in its pejorative sense. He did not dispute Babeuf's belief that the political sentiments held by a 'misled, indoctrinated and ignorant populace are not to be regarded as the people's real will, and that the establishment of a "real Republic" involved acting (and writing) against the majority'. Indeed, as I shall presently show, this is very much Marcuse's own opinion. Even so, Marcuse wrote at the end of this short essay: 'a theory and strategy which was quite unrealistic but not utopian in 1796 appears as utterly utopian today'.

Utterly utopian. And yet not too utterly utopian to prevent Marcuse's taking it up, and promoting it in his subsequent writings. The curious thing is that in his later writings, Marcuse's old optimism returned to him. Fortified, perhaps, by the acclaim of rebellious students throughout the world, if not by the interest of

---

1. *Eros and Civilisation*, p. 216.
2. *One-Dimensional Man* (Beacon Press and Routledge, 1964).
3. *One-Dimensional Man*, p. 257.
4. *In Defense of Gracchus Babeuf*, edited by J. A. Scott, with an essay by Herbert Marcuse (University of Massachusetts Press, 1967).

the press, which he despises, Marcuse recovered the spirit which animated *Eros and Civilisation*. But with optimism and utopian aspiration, there also appeared in Marcuse's writings a new vein of impatience, intolerance, and the will to violence, such as often seems to go together with the more hopeful kind of left-wing yearning.[1] Evidence of Marcuse's later state of mind we find in *A Critique of Pure Tolerance*,[2] published in 1966 in a peculiar format, bound in black like a prayer book or missal and perhaps designed to compete with *The Thoughts of Chairman Mao* as devotional reading at student sit-ins. This is Marcuse's most popular work so far, and his most disturbing.

The argument is simple. The ideal of tolerance belongs to the liberal, democratic tradition which has exhausted itself. What Marcuse likes to call liberalist society is based, he says, on a form of domination so subtle that the majority accept and even will their servitude. In such a condition tolerance as traditionally understood serves the cause of domination. Therefore, Marcuse concludes, a new kind of toleration is needed – tolerance of the Left, tolerance of subversion, tolerance of revolutionary violence, but intolerance of the Right, intolerance of existing institutions, intolerance of any opposition to socialism. His words are beautifully candid:

> As to the scope of this tolerance and intolerance, it would extend to the stage of action as well as of discussion and propaganda, of deed as well as of word. . . . The whole post-fascist period is one of clear and present danger. Consequently, true pacification requires the withdrawal of tolerance before the deed, at the stage of communication in word, print and picture. Such extreme suspension of the right of free speech and free assembly is indeed justified only if the whole of society is in extreme danger. I maintain that our society is in such an emergency situation, and that it has become the normal state of affairs.[3]

Marcuse is eager to see this policy of intolerance adopted without delay:

1. See Karl Popper's essay, 'Utopia and Violence', in *Conjectures and Refutations*, Routledge, 1962.
2. *A Critique of Pure Tolerance*. Essays by Robert Paul Wolff, Barrington Moore, Jr., and Herbert Marcuse, Beacon Press, 1966.
3. *A Critique of Pure Tolerance*, p. 109.
   6*

Withdrawal of tolerance from regressive movements *before* they can become active; intolerance even toward thought, opinion and word, and finally, intolerance in the opposite direction, that is, towards the self-styled conservatives, to the political Right – these anti-democratic notions respond to the actual development of the democratic society which has destroyed the basis for universal tolerance. The conditions under which tolerance can again become a liberating and humanising force have still to be created.[1]

I want to examine the stages by which Herbert Marcuse reached the point of uttering these aggressively illiberal propositions. From one perspective they are not what might have been expected of him. For Marcuse is a scholar, a thinker, and a Jewish refugee from Nazi Germany, a man whose experiences might have been expected to breed some appreciation of that 'liberalist' society which resisted Nazism.

Yet on the other hand there may be readers who would find nothing in Marcuse surprising. For Marcuse is, or claims to be, an Hegelian; and in the historical accounts of Hobhouse, Popper, Camus, and Talmon, Hegel is the central figure in the tradition of German totalitarian fanaticism, so that the Hegelian Marcuse simply takes his place with Fichte, Marx, Bismarck, Hitler, in that sinister succession. I do not myself believe that Hegel can properly be seen as a forerunner of Hitler. He was a constitutional monarchist, with a firm belief in reason and law. But there is undoubtedly a vulgarized 'Hegelian' tradition which contributed something to the success of both Nazism and Fascism, though little compared to the wholly anti-rational, anti-philosophical passions of the *popolo* and the *Volk*. Marcuse himself published in 1941 a book, *Reason and Revolution*,[2] intended to defend Hegel against the charge of being an originator of 'fascist ideas'; but what price that defence now, when Marcuse himself proclaims opinions more extreme than any that have been ascribed to Hegel by Hegel's most uncharitable critics?

But let us return to the evolution of Marcuse's theories. Of his biography I know little but what is to be found in books of reference:

1. Ibid., p. 111.

2. *Reason and Revolution*, New York, 1941; 2nd edn, Beacon Press, 1960, and Routledge, 1968.

that he was born in Germany in 1898, studied philosophy at Berlin and Freiburg, was active in the revolutionary movement of Rosa Luxemburg, one of the several extreme left-wing groups in Germany, which each contributed their share to the destruction of 'bourgeois democracy' in the Weimar Republic. In the academic sphere, Marcuse helped to found (with Max Horkheimer and T. W. Adorno) the 'Frankfurt School' of Marxist sociology, left Germany in 1933 to work at the Institute of Social Research in Geneva, then emigrated to America, where he has been either a research fellow or a professor at Columbia, Harvard, Brandeis, and California universities. In this essay I am concerned only with the ideas set forth in his published works. The earliest one to which he himself appears to attach importance, naming it in the bibliography of *Reason and Revolution*, is one entitled *'Der Kampf gegen der Liberalismus in der totalitären Staatsauffassung'* which was published in Paris in 1935 in the *Zeitschrift für Sozialforschung*,[1] a journal connected with the 'Frankfurt School' of sociology.

This is an essay which throws an important light on Marcuse's subsequent thinking. In the course of it he notes that exponents of Nazi, fascist, and related 'heroic-*völkisch*' irrationalist political ideologies all write bitterly against liberalism. But Marcuse suggests that these attacks are deceptive. For liberalism, he alleges, is deeply connected with fascism and the related creeds. Not only is liberalism 'at one with fascism in its fight against Marxian socialism,' which is the common enemy of both liberalism and fascism, the relationship is in truth more intimate. Liberalism, Marcuse writes, has to be understood as the ideology of capitalism in its competitive phase; when capitalism reaches the monopolistic stage, its ideology changes; and fascism is nothing other than liberalism transfigured to meet the need of an altered economic situation. Elsewhere, in his exposition of Hegel's political theory, Marcuse asserts that 'the gist of Hegel's analysis' of the development of the several stages of government is that 'liberal society necessarily gives birth to an authoritarian state.' (Hegel said nothing so crude). In this German essay, Marcuse advances as his own conclusion that 'it is liberalism that "produces"

1. This essay, with other early writings of Marcuse, has been reproduced in translation in *Negations*, Beacon Press and Allen Lane The Penguin Press, 1968.

the total-authoritarian state out of itself, as its own consummation at a more advanced stage of development'; and he gives as 'evidence' in support of this conclusion what he does not blush to describe as 'a classic document illustrating the inner relationship between liberalist social theory and the (apparently so anti-liberal) totalitarian theory or state: a letter addressed to Mussolini by Gentile when the latter joined the Fascist Party, (saying) "a genuine liberal . . . must enrol in the legion of your followers." '

This view of the relationship between liberalism and fascism, perverse as it is, and jejune, and at variance with all the testimony of history, Marcuse has never retracted, and his continued adherence to it does much to explain the peculiarity of his later theories.

Another significant clue to the working of Marcuse's mind may be found in the pages of *Reason and Revolution*, towards the end of the book, where he discusses the Victorian English Idealist philosopher, Bernard Bosanquet, and his *Philosophical Theory of the State* (1899):

The principles of liberalism [Marcuse writes] are valid; the common interest cannot be other in the last analysis than the product of the multitude of freely developing individual selves in society. But the concrete forms of society that have developed since the nineteenth century have increasingly frustrated the freedom to which liberalism counsels allegiance. Under the laws that govern the social process, the free play of private initiative has wound up in competition among monopolies for the most part . . . Bosanquet's *Philosophical Theory of the State* appeared when this transition from liberal to monopolistic capitalism had already begun. Social theory was faced with the alternative either of abandoning the principles of liberalism so that the existing social order might be maintained, or of fighting the system in order to preserve the principles. The latter choice was implied in the Marxian theory of society.[1]

This last sentence is crucial. Marcuse is saying that the principles of liberalism – freedom, individuality, progress – are good principles, but that liberalism which has always been willing to sacrifice them to defend property and the *status quo*, has now, in turning fascist, abandoned them entirely, while Marxian socialism has taken

1. *Reason and Revolution*, pp. 397–8.

them over, and, unlike liberalism, is willing to do what is needed to uphold liberal principles in the twentieth century, namely, to overthrow existing society.

It is interesting to notice the date of the book in which Marcuse said all this. *Reason and Revolution* was written in 1940 and published in 1941, the years of the great Nazi-Soviet embrace, when *Humanité* tried to obtain a licence to publish in Paris under German auspices, the *G.P.U.* was handing over Jews and other anti-Nazis to the Gestapo in Poland, and the only state effectively resisting Hitler and Mussolini was the homeland of liberal capitalism – and of Bernard Bosanquet – the British Empire. To have asserted *at that time* that Marxian socialism was the true custodian of liberal values, and to have repeated that Marxian socialism not liberalism was fascism's real enemy was surely to betray a remarkable unresponsiveness to the realities of the external world. However, such an unresponsiveness is, as we shall see, an enduring characteristic of Marcuse's mind and method.

It should be said at once that Marcuse's Marxism is not that of the Communist Party. In his book *Soviet Marxism*[1] he describes the prevailing Russian ideology as a genuine form of Marxism. 'The Stalinist reconstruction of Soviet society based itself on Leninism, which was a specific interpretation of Marxian theory and practice', Marcuse writes, but he criticizes that 'reconstruction' because of its totalitarianism and its repressiveness. There are times when he seems to regard the Soviet Union as simply another modern industrial society like the United States, objectionable for the same reasons. Now and again he suggests that the Soviet Union as a totalitarian system is even worse than America, or any democratic system, however defective: '... for the administered individual, pluralistic administration is far better than total administration. One institution might protect him against the other; one organisation might mitigate the impact of the other: possibilities of escape and redress can be calculated. The rule of law, no matter how restricted, is still infinitely safer than the rule above or without law.[2]

1. *Soviet Marxism: a critical analysis* (Routledge, 1958).
2. *One-Dimensional Man*, pp. 50–1.

Marcuse's hostility[1] to totalitarian socialism goes together, reasonably enough, with his belief that Marxism has taken over from liberalism the principles that liberalism has forsaken, notably freedom and individualism. Indeed Marcuse's 'Marxism' embodies principles even more advanced than those. His optimistic belief that a non-repressive civilization is a possibility belongs less to liberalism than to anarchism. If a name had to be chosen for Marcuse's politics it would have to be 'Anarcho-Marxism'.

The reader who can relish irony as well as paradox may venture to consider what Marx himself might have thought of such a conjunction. For Marx met anarchism in the person of Michael Bakhunin, his greatest rival for leadership of the Workers' International, and he hated it; he spoke of anarchism with the liveliest scorn. Bakhunin believed in the possibility of a non-repressive civilization, and he anticipated much that is to be found in the writings of Marcuse. Anarcho-Marxism is a fusion with Marxism of views that Marx himself regarded as wholly antithetical to his own. Marx in his tomb can have felt no qualms when the Spanish Communists in 1938 turned their guns on the Spanish Anarchists; if he was disturbed when the black-and-red flag was unfurled beside the red flag above the Sorbonne in 1968, he could doubtless forgive Daniel Cohn-Bendit and his friends for voicing the eternal desire of youth to have one's cake and eat it; but what Marx would say of Marcuse is something to baffle the imagination.

A certain discretion, or delicacy of feeling, prompts Marcuse to expound his anarchist views most fully, not in his writings on Marx, but in his book on Freud. His argument in *Eros and Civilisation* is a revision of Freud which Marcuse takes care to distinguish from the

1. 'Hostility' is perhaps too strong a word. In a television interview (*Listener*, 17 Oct. 1968), R. T. McKenzie asked Marcuse: 'Is it of concern to you, as a kind of neo-Marxist, that there doesn't seem to be any society based on Marxist-Leninist principles which so far has gotten near the idea of complete freedom of inquiry and debate?'

Marcuse replied: 'It may sound fantastic, but I do not take that as an invalidation of the idea of socialism. We can very well explain the reasons why this has been: under the conditions of so-called peaceful coexistence the construction of socialism is burdened with a huge defence budget which makes it practically impossible to take the direct route to socialism.'

fashionable 'revisionist' or Neo-Freudian theories. Thus, whereas Erich Fromm, Karen Horney and the others seek to add a sociological dimension to the Freudian image of man, Marcuse claims to find the sociological and historical insight in Freud's own theory. He accuses the Neo-Freudians of distorting and emasculating Freud; of taking the sting out of Freud's own judgement on civilization. The aim of their therapy, he says, is to make the patient adjust himself to the world as it is, and even though they may assign to society some of the blame for what is wrong, they treat the individual as the one who is really at fault. Marcuse adds: 'To the Neo-Freudian revisionist, the brute fact of societal repression has transformed itself into a "moral problem" – as it has done in conformist philosophy of all ages.'

I shall not go into the question of whether this attack is just. Erich Fromm, in particular, being himself a New Left personality, might well consider it unjust. I shall simply note that Marcuse addresses to the Neo-Freudian revisionists the same objection that ordinary Marxists use against Freud himself. Freud, they assert, fails to see neurosis as evidence of a sick society; but finding the defect in the individual, seeks to correct it by changing the individual while leaving society untouched. The ordinary Marxists reinforce this criticism by reference to Freud's known political views: Freud was as conservative as Thomas Hobbes, and for much the same reasons, namely that men were in such danger from the violence of human aggression that they would be wise to cling to whatever traditional defences they had. On this view, Freud's own psychoanalysis is, in Marcuse's phrase, 'a conformist philosophy'.

Marcuse offers a different reading of Freud; and by a method which he calls 'extrapolation', or an unfolding of the 'hidden implications' of Freud's theory, he attempts to develop a synthesis of psychoanalysis and socialism. It is Freud in his most cheerless moments that Marcuse fastens on to sustain his most optimistic conclusions. He protests that everyone takes for granted Freud's view that civilization is based on the permanent subjugation of the human instincts, but that no one takes seriously enough Freud's question whether civilization is worth what it has cost in suffering inflicted on individuals. Marcuse quotes Freud's words: 'Happiness is not a cultural value.' Happiness lies in the free gratification of men's instinctual needs, which is incompatible with civilized society. The methodical sacrifice of libido, its rigidly enforced deflection to socially useful activities, *is* culture.

Because Freud speaks in these terms, Marcuse sees him as a profound and far-reaching critic of civilization *as we know it*. At the same time Marcuse argues that Freud's theory provides reasons for rejecting Freud's own conclusion that culture as such necessarily depends on repression as he defines it. Briefly Marcuse's argument is as follows: Freud establishes that some degree of repression is necessary to any civilization, but the extent of repression employed in the actual cultures known to history is far in excess of the amount that Freud shows to be necessary for civilization as such to exist. In fact, Marcuse suggests, 'repressiveness is perhaps the more vigorously maintained the more unnecessary it becomes'. Marcuse then goes on to divide the concept of repression into what he calls *basic* repression and *surplus* repression. The *basic* repressions are the modifications of the human instincts that are necessary (and Marcuse agrees with Freud that some modifications at least are necessary) for the preservation of the human race in civilization. *Surplus* repression comprises the restrictions needed for another purpose. And it is not difficult to guess what that purpose is. It is to maintain the social or class domination which characterizes known societies. On the basis of this distinction, Marcuse puts forward both as realistic and as good Freudian sense his own belief that a non-repressive culture is possible – a non-repressive culture being understood as one from which surplus repression has been eliminated. And if anyone should suggest that civilization would still be, in a very real sense, repressive so long as basic repression remained, Marcuse's answer is that once surplus repression is removed, human instincts themselves will begin to change, so that even basic repression will lose its importance.

The second modification that Marcuse introduces into Freudian psychology concerns the reality principle. Freud himself contrasted the reality principle with the pleasure principle and suggested that as the original animal instinctive man (seeking immediate satisfactions, joy, and liberty) is transformed by culture into a self-controlled mature human (seeking security, accepting delayed satisfactions, restraint, and work), so the reality principle takes the place of the pleasure principle as a man's governing value. Marcuse argues that this reality principle is not something biological or universal, but something to be understood in sociological and historical terms, for it is society, he says, which dictates the sacrifices and restraints that the individual must accept.

'The external world faced by the growing ego is at any stage a specific sociohistorical organization of reality, affecting the mental structure through specific societal agencies or agents,' Marcuse writes, and he goes on to insist that however much Freud may justify the repressive organization of the instincts on the grounds that the primary pleasure principle is irreconcilable with the reality principle, Freud at least 'expresses the historical fact that civilization has progressed as organized *domination*'.

Marcuse continues: 'The "unhistorical" character of the Freudian concepts thus contains the element of its opposite: their historical substance must be recaptured, not by adding some sociological factors (as do the "cultural" Neo-Freudian schools) but by unfolding their own contents.' This task of unfolding – or extrapolation – Marcuse executes with the aid of a terminology unknown to Freud, but based on Freudian language. And just as he divides repression into 'basic' and 'surplus', so he now distinguishes the reality principle from what he calls the '*performance principle*'. His suggestion is that the reality principle takes different forms in different types of society (depending, as he puts it, on the 'mode of domination'); and he calls the form of reality principle which has governed the growth of our own civilization, the 'performance principle' in order (as he explains) 'to emphasize that under its rule society is stratified according to the competitive economic performances of its members'.

Thus, with a brisk audacity, Marcuse uses this notion of a performance principle to marry psychoanalysis to socialism:

The performance principle, which is that of an acquisitive antagonistic society in the process of constant expansion, presupposes a long development during which domination has been increasingly rationalised; control over social labour now reproduces society on an enlarged scale and under improving conditions. For a long way, the interests of domination and the interests of the whole coincide; the profitable utilisation of the productive apparatus fulfils the needs and faculties of the individuals. For the vast majority of the population, the scope and mode of satisfaction is determined by their own labour; but their labour is work for an apparatus which they do not control, which operates as an independent power to which individuals must submit if they want to live. And it becomes the more alien the more specialised the division of labour becomes. Men do not live their own lives, but perform pre-established functions. While they work, they do not fulfil their own needs and faculties, but work in *alienation*.[1]

This marriage, or synthesis, is not intended to yield any therapeutic technique. As the author explains, his aim is to contribute to the philosophy of psychoanalysis, not to psychoanalysis itself, and in his preface he suggests that the traditional frontiers between psychology and political or social theory have been 'made obsolete by the condition of man in the present era'. To put it rather more plainly, Marcuse's purpose is ideological. He holds that most of the repressions sustained in existing society are 'surplus', serving only the interests of politicial domination; further, that men can not only *afford to* throw off these surplus repressions, but their own condition is one of such hellish alienation that they *ought* to do so. What Marcuse holds out is a promise of liberty.

Marcuse not only thinks this revolutionary development conceivable, he even indicates the manner of its realization. Very much like Fourier, to whom he addresses a word of acknowledgement, Marcuse envisages the transformation of labour into pleasure as the solution to the problem of alienation. Again, like Fourier, Marcuse believes that this can be achieved only by a complete change in social institutions, a distribution of the social product according to need, the assignment of functions according to talent and the provision of 'attractive labour'. Marcuse praises Fourier for having noticed that the possibility of *le travail attrayant* 'derives above all from the release of libidinal forces', but he criticizes Fourier for having proposed an authoritarian socialist community which retained the repressive element. Marcuse's objection to Fourier is Bakhunin's

1. *Eros and Civilisation*, p. 41.

objection, enlivened with a dressing of sex. Marcuse suggests that *le travail attrayant* is possible only if work is transformed into play; and work as free play 'cannot be subject to administration.' He continues: 'If pleasure is indeed in the act of working and not extraneous to it, such pleasure must be derived from the acting organs of the body and the body itself, activating the erotogenic zones or eroticizing the body as a whole; in other words, it must be libidinal pleasure.'[1]

It is necessary at this point to remember that Marcuse sees as one essential feature of a non-repressive civilization a change in the nature of sexuality itself. He thinks it important to demonstrate that the sexual instincts can, by virtue of their own dynamic, generate under changed social conditions lasting erotic relationships and even promote progress towards higher forms of civilized freedom. He is careful to explain that the social changes he has in mind involve not simply a release, but a transformation of the libido, a transformation 'from sexuality constrained under genital supremacy to erotization of the entire personality'.

It is a spread rather than an explosion of libido – a spread over private and societal relations which bridges the gap maintained between them by a repressive reality principle. This transformation of the libido would be the result of a societal transformation that released the free play of individual needs and faculties. By virtue of these conditions the free development of transformed libido *beyond* the institutions of the performance principle differs essentially from the release of unconstrained sexuality *within* the dominion of these institutions. The latter process explodes *suppressed* sexuality; the libido continues to bear the mark of suppression and manifests itself in the hideous forms so well known in the history of civilisation; in the sadistic and masochistic orgies of desperate masses, of 'society élites', of starved bands of mercenaries, of prison and concentration camp guards. Such release of sexuality provides a periodically necessary outlet for unbearable frustration; it strengthens rather than weakens the roots of instinctual constraint; consequently, it has been used time and again as prop for suppressive régimes. In contrast the free development of transformed libido within transformed institutions, while eroticising previously tabooed zones, time, and relations would *minimise* the manifestations of *mere* sexuality by integrating them into a far larger

1. Ibid., p. 201.

order, including the order of work. In this context, sexuality tends to its own sublimation: the libido would not simply reactivate pre-civilised and infantile stages, but would also transform the perverted content of these stages.[1]

Here, assuredly, is the voice of optimism; and it is an optimism based entirely on faith, for Marcuse offers no evidence whatsoever to justify his conclusions. The optimists of the eighteenth century at least gave some empirical grounds for their belief that a removal of religious taboos would produce better sexual relationships. They quoted the discovery by Bougainville and other voyagers of primitive societies where sexual freedom and happiness went together. But Marcuse offers nothing of the kind. His method is purely aprioristic. Like Hobbes, 'shut up in his cabinet in the dark', he has no need to study nature; he works everything out in his head. It is a little sum: basic repression plus surplus repression yields a troubled and destructive libido; take away surplus repression and the libido retains only its creative and satisfying elements. The magic word is 'transformation', which is oddly like 'conversion' to religious revivalists of the Puritan tradition. It does not just mean change. It means a total alteration from something thoroughly bad to something thoroughly good. And, of course, this 'transformation' is not an empirical concept at all. It is an intellectual construction, and what it entails depends entirely on the manner in which it is defined.

Marcuse proclaims his attachment to the dialectical method; and the dialectic, in his use of it, turns out to be a kind of conjuror's hat out of which truths can be produced at will: 'When historical content enters into the dialectical concept and determines methodologically its development and function, dialectical thought attains the concreteness which links the structure of thought to that of reality. Logical truth becomes historical truth.'

Fortunately, we are not here concerned with Marcuse as a technical philosopher. Indeed he scarcely attempts to assume this role. He offers, admittedly, a defence of the Hegelian metaphysical style of philosophy against the rival tradition of empiricism and positivism. But his criteria are ideological, rather than philosophical. For

3. Ibid., p. 184.

example, his main objection to positivism is that it serves the interest of conservatism. 'The protagonists and positivism', he writes, 'took great pains to stress the conservative and affirmative attitude of their philosophy; it induces thought to be satisfied with the facts, to renounce any transgression beyond them, and to bow to the given state of affairs.' Correspondingly, Marcuse praises Hegel for holding that 'the facts in themselves possess no authority', and thus preparing the way for what Marcuse considers a truly critical or negative philosophy.

His objections to contemporary logical positivism and linguistic analysis are equally ideological. He even goes so far as to assert that the current techniques of linguistic analysis 'spread the atmosphere of denunciation and investigation by committee. The intellectual is called on the carpet. What do you mean when you say . . .?. Don't you conceal something. . . .?' But, alas, this wild thought is all he adds to stock accusations of methodical triviality against analytic philosophy, and therefore need not detain us.

The nine years which separate *Eros and Civilisation* from Marcuse's next substantial book mark a decline in his spirits. In *One-Dimensional Man*, published in 1964, he is no longer concerned with the possibility of a non-repressive civilization, but rather with the repressiveness of existing, and especially American civilization. Julius Gould reviewed the book in *Encounter* (September 1964), under the title 'The Dialectics of Despair', and Allen Graubard's review in the American Left-wing journal *Dissent* was headed 'One-Dimensional Pessimism'. And it is assuredly a bleak and depressing book; that it has also been a U.S. best-seller may suggest, however, that Americans 'can take it'.

At the heart of this book there lies the belief of Babeuf which I have already mentioned, that 'the political sentiments held by a misled, indoctrinated and ignorant populace are not to be regarded as the people's real will and that the establishment of a "real Republic" involves acting (and writing) against the people, against the majority'. Marcuse in *One-Dimensional Man* sets out to show just how misled, indoctrinated, ignorant and indeed corrupted are the people, the majority, in modern industrialized societies. The only society he describes is America, and although he nowhere distinguishes between industrial society in general and the United States in particular, he may be assumed to consider America to be the archetype of such civilization, and the model towards which all other industrial societies are moving.

Just as he elsewhere attacks liberalism for betraying its own principles, he here attacks modern democracy as a fraudulent system of popular government, vitiated by the perversion of people's minds, and even their souls, by modern techniques of domination. We are never told precisely who dominates, but there are several vague references to vested interests, the Establishment, the ruling classes and the rich. Domination in the abstract is what is usually complained of. However, domination is seen as a characteristic of all known societies, and Marcuse's particular objection to the modern democratic system is that it makes the people mistake their servitude for liberty, and like it.

Affluence itself has corrupted men. Today 'people recognize themselves in their commodities; they find their soul in their automobile, hi-fi set, split-level home, kitchen equipment'. The very productive apparatus, the goods and services which modern society produces 'sell' or impose the social system on the people: 'The means of mass transportation and communication, the commodities of lodging, food and clothing, the irresistible output of the entertainment and information industry carry with them prescribed attitudes and habits, certain intellectual and emotional reactions which bind the consumers more or less pleasantly to the producers and, through the latter, to the whole.[1] In this way, as Marcuse puts it, the spread of the material products of industrialization to more and more people means that 'the indoctrination they carry ceases to be publicity; it becomes a way of life.'

He is ready to admit that this way of life may seem to be *better* than that which preceded the rise of industrialization even as the Welfare State may seem to be an improvement on previous arrangements. But Marcuse holds that neither form of betterment is genuine because each diminishes the desire for revolution, each 'militates against qualitative change'. Indeed Marcuse goes so far

1. *One-Dimensional Man*, p. 12.

as to speak of 'those whose life is the hell of the Affluent Society' and he asserts that such people are 'kept in line by a brutality which revives medieval and early modern practices'. He enlarges on this last remark by describing the inhabitants of the Affluent Society as slaves: 'The slaves of developed industrial civilization are sublimated slaves, but they are slaves, for slavery is determined "neither by obedience nor by hardness of labour but by the status of being a mere instrument, and the reduction of man to the status of a thing".'[1]

In the Affluent Society, moreover, liberty itself is made into 'a perfect instrument of domination'; for the freedom it affords is no more than free competition at administered prices, a free press that censors itself, free choice between brands and gadgets. 'Free election of masters', he adds, 'does not abolish the masters and the slaves. Free choice among a wide variety of goods and services does not signify freedom, if those goods and services . . . sustain alienation.' As for the equality of which modern American society at any rate boasts, it is just as spurious, according to Marcuse, just as inimical to real equality as its so-called liberty is inimical to real liberty:

If the worker and his boss enjoy the same television programme and visit the same resort places, if the typist is as attractively made-up as the daughter of her employer, if the Negro owns a Cadillac, if they all read the same newspaper, then this assimilation indicates not the disappearances of classes, but the extent to which the needs and satisfactions that serve the preservation of the Establishment are shared by the underlying population.[2]

In the 'hell of the Affluent Society' people have lost the spiritual qualities they possessed in simpler and less prosperous societies, lost even the capacity they had for sexual experience:

Compare love-making in a meadow and in an automobile, on a lovers' walk outside the town walls and on a Manhattan street. In the former cases the environment partakes of and invites libidinal cathexis and tends to be eroticised. Libido transcends beyond the immediate erotogenic zones – a process of non-repressive sublimation. In contrast, a mechanised environment seems to block such self-transcendence of libido.

1. *One-Dimensional Man*, pp. 32–3. (The words in quotation marks are taken from the French of François Perroux.)
2. Ibid., p. 8.

To Marcuse the so-called sexual freedom of modern permissive society is simply another fraud; it is even worse than the old taboos because such 'greater liberty involves a contraction rather than extension and development of instinctual needs ... it works *for* rather than *against* the *status quo* of general repression'.

Worst of all, industrial society has killed the urge to resistance. The class war between bourgeoisie and workers has ended not only in 'collusion' between the labour unions and the employers, but in a reconciliation of the workers to their own condition; they are all so well off in their own eyes that they can no longer act as 'agents of historical transformation'. Workers and bourgeois, united by their desire to preserve existing institutions, suffer from the same disease, the Hegelian 'happy consciousness', a form of comfortable self-deception about their own true interests; they believe that productivity, industrial output, more and more consumer goods are to everyone's advantage. 'The technological controls appear to be the very embodiment of Reason for the benefit of all social groups and interests – to such an extent that all contradiction seems irrelevant and all counteraction impossible.' Moreover, 'the intellectual and emotional refusal to go along appears neurotic and impotent.' This is the most lamentable feature of the present era: 'the passing of the historical forces which, at the preceding stage of industrial society, seemed to represent the possibility of new forms of existence.'

The corrupted mind of the modern man allows him, Marcuse notes with bitterness, to accept without protest preparations for nuclear war, the falsehoods and vulgarity of advertising, and the built-in obsolescence of automobiles. Intellectuals are as much affected by the process as the rest of society. The *homo conformans* of modern society is a 'one-dimensional man', one who follows 'a pattern of one-dimensional thought and behaviour in which ideas, aspirations and objectives that by their content transcend the established universe of discourse and action are either repelled or reduced to the terms of this universe'. The missing dimension is the dimension of critical awareness or 'negative' thinking.

Language itself is corrupted. Marcuse speaks of the illogicality and ugliness of style in a typical *Time* news item, and contrasts it (somewhat as he contrasts love-making in a meadow and in cars) with the classical literary and logical qualities exhibited by (of all things) *The Communist Manifesto*. The style of modern journalism and publicity has, and seeks to have, a hypnotic effect. Its aim is not communication from mind to mind, but the 'overwhelming' of the reader's consciousness. And in its most sophisticated form, the effect of this hypnotic language is that 'people don't believe it, or don't care and yet act accordingly'. *Homo conformans* is not a fool; he is not deceived by others; his misfortune is that he deceives himself. One-dimensional man is his own creation.

In such a situation, the difference between modern democratic and totalitarian systems diminishes:

By virtue of the way it has organised its technological base, contemporary industrial society tends to be totalitarian. For 'totalitarianism' is not only a terroristic political coordination of society, but also a nonterroristic economic technical coordination which operates through the manipulation of needs by vested interests. It thus precludes the emergence of an effective opposition against the whole. Not only a specific form of government or party rule makes for totalitarianism, but also a specific system of production and distribution which may well be compatible with a 'pluralism' of parties, newspapers, 'countervailing powers,' etc.[1]

Here presumably is another dialectical transformation: as liberalism turns itself into fascism, democracy turns itself into totalitarianism.

What are the prospects of redemption? In *One-Dimensional Man* Marcuse scarcely considers them. It follows from his diagnosis that modern industrial civilization is getting worse and not better, and that the most charmless features of the most advanced of modern societies are likely to be reproduced in the others as they catch up. Even so, Marcuse does discern one faint ray of hope, one slender possibility of a revolutionary movement emerging.

On his penultimate page, he writes:

... underneath the conservative popular base is the substratum of the outcasts and outsiders, the exploited and the persecuted of other races and other colours, the unemployed and the unemployable. They exist outside the democratic process, their life is the most immediate and the most real

1. Ibid., p. 3.

need for ending intolerable conditions and institutions. Thus their opposition is revolutionary even if their consciousness is not. Their opposition hits the system from without and is therefore not deflected by the system; it is an elementary force that violates the rules of the game. ... The fact that they start refusing to play the game may be the fact which marks the beginning of the end of a period.[1]

Marcuse adds candidly: 'Nothing indicates that it will be a good end.' And his book closes on a mournful note. But since he published *One-Dimensional Man* in 1964 this idea that salvation might come through 'outsiders' has evidently blossomed in his mind. It is, of course, the same idea that Sartre and others hold of a 'new proletariat' being constituted by the *damnés de la terre*, the coloured races, 'the victims of neo-colonialism' and such-like to perform the historic revolutionary mission which the prosperous Western working classes have abandoned. This 'New Proletariat' of Outsiders is also one with which *déraciné* intellectuals and students[2] readily identify themselves; for it is a proletariat which is at the same time an élite. On Marcuse's analysis it must be one, since the majority is in such a pitiful condition. The 'vast majority accepts, and is made to accept' prevailing values; and does not know the difference between 'true and false consciousness'.

Marcuse's argument is neatly summed up in this paragraph:

In the last analysis, the question of what is true and false needs to be answered by the individuals themselves, *but only in the last analysis*: that is, if and when they are free to give their own answer. As long as they are kept incapable of being autonomous, as long as they are indoctrinated and manipulated (down to their very instincts) *their answer to this question cannot be taken as their own.*[3]

1. Ibid., pp. 256–7.
2. Discussing student protests on television, R. T. McKenzie had this exchange with Marcuse (*Listener*, 17 October 1968): 'I have the uncomfortable feeling that a certain section of the student movement is committed to a wrecking operation.' 'I think that is a minority. I do not identify myself with it, although I would not discard their activities as merely a wrecking operation.' 'Are you arguing there can be no enemy to the left?' 'The left is such that an enemy on the left is rather hard to imagine. We have so many enemies on the right.'
3. Ibid., p. 6 (my italics).

Marcuse's theory of toleration, as set forth in *A Critique of Pure Tolerance*, follows logically from this position. Toleration, as one need hardly say, is regarded as a virtue in all liberal and democratic societies. And Marcuse professes his assent: tolerance *is* a good thing, it is an end in itself. 'The elimination of violence, and the reduction of suppression to the extent required for protecting men and animals from cruelty and aggression are preconditions for the creation of a human society.' Only, alas, he adds, such a society does not yet exist. In the societies which do exist what is proclaimed and practised as tolerance 'serves the cause of oppression'. Things are tolerated which ought not to be tolerated, and what ought to be tolerated is not tolerated.

Once again Marcuse protests about the hell of the Affluent Society where evil is accepted and even thought to be good so long as it serves the cause of affluence:

The tolerance of the systematic moronisation of children and adults alike by publicity and propaganda, the release of destructiveness in driving, the recruitment for and training of special forces, the impotent and benevolent tolerance towards outright deception in merchandising, waste and planned obsolescence, are not distortions and aberrations, they are the essence of a system which fosters tolerance as a means for perpetuating the struggle for existence and suppressing the alternatives.[1]

Toleration is historically a progressive idea, Marcuse agrees. But, he asserts, 'within a repressive society even progressive movements can have a reactionary effect if they accept the rules of the game.' For example, he suggests that the exercise of citizens' rights in modern so-called democracies, by voting, writing letters to the press, and taking part in *protest-demonstrations with a prior renunciation of counter-violence* (I shall return to this question of violence later), in effect simply 'serves to strengthen repressive administration' by testifying to the existence of non-existent liberties. It is worth remembering that this proposal that socialists should hold aloof from established politics was one of Bakhunin's policies, and one which annoyed Marx exceedingly.

Marcuse believes that the only tolerance worth having is what he

1. *A Critique of Pure Tolerance*, p. 83.

calls 'partisan tolerance'. Any kind of impartial, or non-partisan tolerance simply 'protects the already established system'. The chief characteristic of partisan tolerance is that it is intolerant towards the 'repressive status quo'. Marcuse adds:

> Tolerance cannot be indiscriminate and equal with respect to the contents of expression, neither in word nor deed, it cannot protect false words and wrong deeds which demonstrate that they contradict and counteract the possibilities of liberation. Such indiscriminate tolerance is justified in harmless debates, in conversation, in academic discussion; it is indispensable in scientific enterprise, in private religion. But society cannot be indiscriminate where the pacification of existence, where freedom and happiness themselves are at stake; here, certain things cannot be said, certain ideas cannot be expressed, certain policies cannot be proposed, certain behaviour cannot be permitted without making tolerance an instrument for the continuation of servitude.[1]

Marcuse recalls that the theory of toleration, as put forward by its most philosophical exponents, is based on the assumption that men are rational creatures, capable of seeing the truth for themselves and of discerning their own rights and interests. Such, Marcuse continues, is 'the rationale of free speech and assembly'. But 'universal toleration becomes questionable when its rationale no longer prevails, when tolerance is administered to manipulated and indoctrinated individuals who parrot, as their own, the opinions of their masters, for whom heteronomy has become autonomy . . .'[2]

Precisely because people are thus indoctrinated by the very conditions under which they live, the only way for them to be enabled to distinguish the truth is for them to be freed from this

---

1. Ibid., p. 88.

2. In his B.B.C. television broadcast, Marcuse gave another reason for favouring 'discriminating tolerance', or 'intolerance towards movements from the right, intolerance of movements from the right'. Marcuse explained (*Listener*, 17 October 1968):

'You see, I believe that we have the discriminating tolerance today already, and what I want to do is redress the balance. The Left, and especially the militant Left, lacks the funds that are necessary to be heard in the mass media. They have no newspapers of large circulation, they cannot get any of the larger television networks. So you have a perfectly legal discriminating tolerance already.'

indoctrination. And this, Marcuse does not hesitate to say, means *counter-indoctrination.*

Here we meet the crucial part of his argument. Marcuse does not accept the classical notion that ye shall know the truth and the truth shall set ye free. Biased information can only be corrected by information equally biased. Freeing men from the prevailing indoctrination, Marcuse explains, 'means that the trend would have to be reversed; they would have to get their information slanted in the opposite direction. For the facts are never given immediately and never accessible immediately; they are established, "mediated" by those who made them; the truth, "the whole truth", surpasses these facts and requires the rupture with their appearance.'

Having said this, Marcuse protests that he does not wish to introduce any dictatorship, but only to replace totalitarian democracy with a genuinely free society which would not allow itself to be subverted by a manipulated majority. The 'apparently undemocratic means' – as he calls them – likely to be necessary to promote such a transformation,

include the withdrawal of toleration of speech and assembly from groups and movements which promote aggressive policies, armament, chauvinism, discrimination on the grounds of race and religion, or which opposed the extension of public services, social security, medical care, etc. Moreover, the restoration of freedom of thought may necessitate new and rigid restrictions on teachings and practices in the educational institutions which, by their very methods and concepts, serve to enclose the mind within the established universe of discourse and behaviour.[1]

But who is to articlate and impose these 'rigid restrictions'? Marcuse is disappointingly vague: 'While the reversal of the trend in the educational enterprise could conceivably be enforced by the students and teachers themselves, and thus be self-imposed, the systematic withdrawal of tolerance towards regressive and repressive opinions and movements could only be envisaged as results of large-scale pressure which would amount to an upheaval.'

'Upheaval' is presumably another word for 'revolution'. But what kind of revolution? Again Marcuse cuts off his narrative with

1. Ibid., p. 101.

these difficult questions unanswered: 'The author is fully aware that, at present, no power, no authority, no government exists which would translate liberating tolerance into practice; but he believes that it is the task and duty of the intellectual to recall and preserve historical possibilities which seem to have become utopian possibilities – that it is his task to break the concreteness of oppression in order to open the mental space in which this society can be recognized as what it is and does.'

The one thing that Marcuse does reveal about the upheaval or revolution he desires is that it entails violence. I have already quoted his condemnation of those who participate 'in protest-demonstrations with a prior renunciation of counter-violence'. Marcuse is frank in his scepticism towards the beliefs of the Gandhis and Martin Luther Kings in non-violent resistance.

'To refrain from violence in the face of vastly superior violence is one thing; to renounce *a priori* violence against violence, on ethical or psychological grounds (because it may antagonize sympathizers) is another.' 'Non-violence,' he adds, is 'a necessity rather than a virtue,' and 'normally it does not harm the cause of the strong'.

Like Sartre, Marcuse claims that violence is a feature of all existing régimes. 'Even in the advanced centres of civilization,' Marcuse writes, 'violence actually prevails.' And this to his eyes is bad violence. But violence used *against* the established system is another matter altogether.

In terms of historical function, there is a difference between revolutionary and reactionary violence, between violence practised by the oppressed and by the oppressors. In terms of ethics, both forms of violence are inhuman, and evil – but *since when is history made in accordance with ethical standards*? To start applying them at the point where the oppressed rebel against the oppressors, the have-nots against the haves, is serving the cause of actual violence by weakening the protest against it.[1]

What Marcuse means by 'actual violence' is that force which reinforces law in existing societies; and he goes on to make the bold suggestion that the chances of human progress seem 'to involve the calculated choice between two forms of political violence; that on the

1. Ibid., p. 103 (my italics).

part of the legally constituted powers ... and that on the part of potentially subversive movements'. He asks: 'Can the historical calculus be reasonably extended to the justification of one form of violence against another?' There is not much doubt in his answer: 'With all the qualifications of a hypothesis based on an "open" historical record, it seems that violence emanating from the rebellion of the oppressed classes broke the historical continuum of injustice, cruelty and silence for a brief moment, brief but explosive enough to achieve an increase in the scope of freedom and justice and ... progress in civilization.'[1]

In short Marcuse holds that so long as violence comes from below, from the 'oppressed', it is acceptable. And he thinks history gives him rational grounds for this conclusion. His conception of what actually happened in history is admittedly odd. Our modern civilization, he fancies, 'was painfully born in the violence of the heretic revolts of the thirteenth century and the peasant and labourer revolts of the fourteenth century'. But Marcuse's history is less worrying than the conclusions, the moral conclusions, which he uses his history to sustain.

I have been concerned in this essay more to expound Marcuse's theories than to criticize them, although I will confess that I think that one has only to set forth clearly the main lines of his thinking to reveal it as being at once nugatory and dangerous. It is nugatory because it rests on premises which cannot be justified, and because it is developed by arguments which serve only to enlarge its defects. It is dangerous because it advocates intolerance and confers a blessing on violence. While paying lip-service to reason and truth, Marcuse appeals continuously to passion and recommends what can only be called the bending of truth to the service of a revolutionary end.

The analytic devices he introduces are worthless. His distinction, for example, between basic and surplus repression is no aid to understanding because he gives us no means of telling what surplus repression it. There is really no room for discussion here. Nobody believes in surplus repression, because the word 'surplus' means, by defini-

1. Ibid., p. 107.

tion, that which is in excess of what is needed. And even a Stalin could say he did not believe in having any more repression than was needed, though he had different ideas of what was needed than others might have. Assuredly, Marcuse offers some explanation of what he himself considers surplus repression, namely that repression which is needed to uphold 'class domination'. But this does not help us, because the most repressive societies known to history have either been wholly classless, as in the case of the U.S.S.R., or almost classless, as was the Third Reich. The most class-dominated societies, such as England in the eighteenth century, have sometimes been the least repressive. Of course, the word 'repression' is itself so loaded, so pejorative, that it sounds odd to speak in favour of any kind of repression at all. And this was one of Freud's misfortunes, that writing in ordinary language, he had to use words that were not scientific or neutral or *wertfrei* as he would have liked them to be, but which had a heavy evaluative content, so to speak, built into them. Freud met this difficulty, not altogether successfully, by developing a quasitechnical vocabulary of his own. Marcuse, by contrast, ignores the difficulty. And as a result his style is a curious mixture of quasitechnical terms and ideological jargon, of rhetoric and everyday language.

And then, in addition to the distinctions that Marcuse makes uselessly, there are the distinctions that he refuses to acknowledge. For example, violence is never distinguished from force. The only difference that Marcuse recognizes is that between revolutionary and reactionary violence. He thus banishes the simple, but very important, distinction between the force, or strong arm, seldom actually used, of the law and the aggressive infliction of injury or damage which is violence in the common understanding of the word. 'Violence' is another word which has an element of censure incorporated in its meaning; 'force' is a word with a distinctively different use; force is not by definition immoderate. And Marcuse's manner of lumping together legitimate force and terrorism in the same category of violence is to make nonsense of the whole conception of the rule of law, which is nevertheless a phrase that he himself employs.

In a similar way, Marcuse's indiscriminate use of the word

'totalitarian', whether for such countries as the Soviet Union or for the United States, robs the word 'totalitarian' of any utility. For quite apart from the relative merits of Russia and America, their objectively verifiable methods of government are so vastly different that any one word which describes them both equally well is bound to be a word that tells us very little about either.

But what is perhaps the most ruinous defect of Marcuse's whole anarcho-Marxist theory is that it combines the worst features of both anarchism and Marxism, with few of the merits of either. This comes out most clearly in the means he recommends to achieve his libertarian ends. For it is not that he proposes, in the manner of Bakhunin and the nineteenth-century anarchists, simply to destroy the old system by burning down government buildings and so forth. Such destructive *élan*, however lamentable one may personally consider it, is not inconsistent with a demand for the abolition of all government. But Marcuse asks for more than this. He calls not only for terror, but for a reign of terror. He asks for the suppression of conservatives, for the suppression of conservative speech, even of conservative thought. This calls for the creation of institutions of suppression which must exist for as long as conservative thoughts are likely to continue to exist in anyone's mind. Marcuse is therefore calling for something uncannily like the State-that-is-to-wither-away (but not wither away very soon) which is at once the most conspicuous and the most charmless feature of orthodox Marxist ideology. For all his attacks on Stalinism, Marcuse himself is calling for the very things that make Stalinism odious. And let us not be led astray by Marcuse's constant avowal of his attachment to the idea of freedom; as Milton and Locke remarked in the seventeenth century, the people who talk most about liberty are frequently its greatest enemies.

In seeking to distinguish the main lines of his argument and the principle of coherence which unifies his work, I have withheld attention from one feature which ought not to be neglected. Marcuse presents himself so determinedly as a Hegelian rationalist, he goes on and on so much about reason, that one almost forgets to remark how much he is a man of feeling. *Eros and Civilisation* is a highly

7

romantic work. The best chapters are those devoted to poetry and aesthetics, where the author speaks of the need for 'the self-sublimation of sensuousness' as the way to creation of a free culture, the same idea that was advanced with such valiant repetitiveness by the late Sir Herbert Read, who recognized that it belonged to romanticism and not to rationalism. Marcuse writes with a remarkable sympathy about Schiller, Rilke and Baudelaire; in the world of literature and mythology, he is clearly at ease and at home.

This is not to say that he gives the impression of exercising to a marked degree the faculty of imagination. In all his strictures on the Affluent Society and the welfare state, he never enters for one moment the mind of the working man in the real world, to whom the dawn of prosperity after years of unemployment and recession meant an immense step forward from woeful deprivation to a decent condition of life; or the minds of those afflicted and needy people to whom social services have brought such signal relief. To Marcuse the past means making love in meadows in an age when a gentlemanly life was still possible. His attitude to the present world is often indistinguishable from that of any elderly Blimp or Junker:

The degree to which the population is allowed to break the peace wherever there is still peace and silence, to be ugly and uglify things, to ooze familiarity, to offend against good form is frightening. It is frightening because it expresses the lawful and even organized effort to reject the Other in his own right, to prevent autonomy even in a small, reserved sphere of existence. In the over-developed countries, an ever-larger part of the population becomes one huge captive audience — captured not by a totalitarian régime, but by the liberties of the citizens whose media of amusement and elevation compel the Other to partake of their sounds, sights and smells.[1]

I have put this paragraph in italics because I conceive it to be the key passage not only to *One-Dimensional Man*, but to Marcuse's whole attitude. He often uses the word *alienation*. Alienation is the central theme of the Marxism he expounded as long ago as 1941 in *Reason and Revolution*; he might even claim with Georg Lukács the honour of having introduced the word into Left-wing conversation.

---

1. *One-Dimensional Man*, pp. 244–5.

But it is also a word that can be aptly applied to Marcuse's own predicament. His feelings about the real world, towards the 'repressive civilization' which is the only kind of civilization we know, towards 'domination', which is the only kind of political order we have, are manifestly alienated. Far more than his divine discontent and moral disapproval towards the inhabitants of the modern world, one is conscious of a simple disgust. The people, the populace, the majority, are manipulated, indoctrinated, enslaved; Marcuse cannot bear their sights, their sounds, their smells.

And here, of course, he is very unlike Bakhunin, the Russian nobleman who adored the simple people, and detected in the honest sweat of labourers the true scent of human excellence. Marcuse has more German instincts, recoiling from the *Untermenschen*. In a interview in Venice given in 1968 to an Italian magazine Marcuse said that Venice ought to be reserved for high-class tourism only (*un turismo di qualità*), and that the *hoi polloi* who disturbed its solemn beauty should be kept out.[1] The idea of mankind appeals to him; real men – most of them – sicken him. For this reason it is as difficult to believe in his anarchism as it is, for other reasons, to believe in his Marxism. Marcuse's 'negative philosophy' is assuredly negative; his 'negations' are real negations, and not in the fanciful sense for which he claims the authority of Hegel; but in the ordinary sense of rejection or denial of the positive. Ideologists march, like soldiers, on their stomachs; and Marcuse has the stomach of a very high-class aesthete, queasy, fastidious, and misanthropic.

1. *Il Tempo*, August 1968, p. 17.

Index